Preston Sprinkle introduces us to the real Jesus of the Bible and to his way of life that changes everything. With strong biblical insight and practical wisdom, *Go: Returning Discipleship to the Front Lines of Faith* is a must-read.

BRANDON HATMAKER
Founder of the Legacy Collective and author of *A Mile Wide* and *Barefoot Church*

In typical Preston Sprinkle fashion, he invites us to discover a newfound joy in the disciple-making Jesus longs for in his church. As leaders wrestle with generations abandoning faith, this resource is acute—full of insight and the truth that leads to deep transformation.

GABE LYONS
Author of *Good Faith* and founder of Q Ideas

Sadly, many of our modern-day definitions of "discipleship" focus on a personal (and primarily inward-focused) relationship with Jesus that has little to do with the deeply communal nature of the New Testament church. In *Go: Returning Discipleship to the Front Lines of Faith*, Preston Sprinkle offers a much-needed counterbalance to the rugged spiritual individualism of our age. He presents a definition and path of discipleship that engages the entire church and, more importantly, aligns with the definition and path of discipleship found in the New Testament. If you are serious about biblical discipleship, this book is a must-read.

LARRY OSBORNE
Author and pastor of North Coast Church

This is a must-read for anyone wanting to make disciples and ignite a disciple-making movement. Sprinkle does a great job filling in the gaps of many contemporary thoughts on disciple making, and he restores the importance of grace as we invest in others. Along the way, he gives practical helps on how to make your discipleship relationships more authentic and missional. I highly recommend this book!

CRAIG ETHEREDGE
Senior pastor of First Colleyville and author of *Bold Moves*

GO

RETURNING
DISCIPLESHIP TO
THE FRONT LINES
OF FAITH

PRESTON SPRINKLE

NAVPRESS®

*A NavPress resource published in alliance
with Tyndale House Publishers, Inc.*

NavPress is the publishing ministry of The Navigators, an international Christian organization and leader in personal spiritual development. NavPress is committed to helping people grow spiritually and enjoy lives of meaning and hope through personal and group resources that are biblically rooted, culturally relevant, and highly practical.

For more information, visit www.NavPress.com.

Go: Returning Discipleship to the Front Lines of Faith

Copyright © 2016 by The Navigators. All rights reserved.

A NavPress resource published in alliance with Tyndale House Publishers, Inc.

NAVPRESS, the NAVPRESS logo, *THE MESSAGE*, and THE MESSAGE logo are registered trademarks of NavPress, The Navigators, Colorado Springs, CO. *TYNDALE* is a registered trademark of Tyndale House Publishers, Inc. Absence of ® in connection with marks of NavPress or other parties does not indicate an absence of registration of those marks.

Cover photograph copyright © Jim Anness/500px. All rights reserved.

The Team:
Don Pape (Publisher), David Zimmerman (Editor), Mark Lane (Designer)

Published in association with the literary agency of Wolgemuth & Associates, Inc.

Library of Congress Cataloging-in-Publication Data

Names: Sprinkle, Preston M., date, author.
Title: Go : returning discipleship to the front lines of faith / Preston Sprinkle.
Description: Colorado Springs : NavPress, 2016. | Includes bibliographical references.
 | Description based on print version record and CIP data provided by publisher; resource not viewed.
Identifiers: LCCN 2016019892 (print) | LCCN 2016015625 (ebook) | ISBN 9781631466137 (Apple) | ISBN 9781631466113 (E-Pub) | ISBN 9781631466120 (Kindle) | ISBN 9781631466106
Subjects: LCSH: Spiritual formation. | Discipling (Christianity)
Classification: LCC BV4511 (print) | LCC BV4511 .S69 2016 (ebook) | DDC 253—dc23
LC record available at https://lccn.loc.gov/2016015625

Printed in the United States of America

22   21   20   19   18   17   16
7   6   5   4   3   2   1

For Francis Chan

Thank you for making the radicalness of following Jesus

look and feel

so normal

so Christian

so impossible

and so right

CONTENTS

FOREWORD

by David Kinnaman

How CAN WE GROW followers of Jesus who love God with their whole heart, mind, soul and strength when nearly every force in our rapidly changing culture seems arrayed against this outcome?

Making and growing disciples is challenging in any setting, but it seems especially tough in a narcissistic and pleasure-seeking age such as ours. For example, one of the prevailing ideas of our time is that people can find the best versions of themselves by looking inside themselves. Nine out of ten US adults (91 percent) and three-quarters of practicing Christians (76 percent) agree with this notion. The idea that the self is the "center of meaning" holds sway over our culture and has gained surprising traction within today's Christian community. Thus, many Christians view *internal inputs*—feelings, perceptions, and so on—as equal to or more valid than *external sources of authority* such as the Bible, church tradition, or the wisdom of their Christian brothers and sisters. This view is the very essence of the lone-wolf, choose-your-own-spiritual-adventure mind-set. *You know what's best for you. Look inside to find yourself and be fulfilled. Be true to yourself.* These lies about humanity have been widely embraced by a selfie-obsessed generation.

The truth of the gospel stands in stark contrast: We find ourselves in a fixed point outside of ourselves, in Jesus Christ revealed by the Scriptures.

Following this Jesus is not a solo pursuit. The practices that shape us into people who love God with our whole selves and our neighbor as ourselves can't be done by lone wolves—yet so many would-be disciples are distracted by the self-centered demands of our age that work against communion with God and others.

True discipleship is the only way out.

Go: Returning Discipleship to the Front Lines of Faith is unique. This is partly because this book is more than the author's opinions. It is informed by a major research study commissioned by The Navigators and undertaken by Barna to explore the current state of discipleship. In other words, what you're going to read isn't just random ideas from a (terrific) guy with theories about discipleship; Preston's observations are anchored in a broader set of findings discovered by Barna researchers. (Learn more about that study and our findings by downloading the full report at http://www.barna. org/discipleship.)

This book is also unique because Preston Sprinkle is just the person to guide us. Uncovering orthodox yet fresh ideas about discipleship requires someone like Preston: willing to ask real questions, to surface unpleasant realities, and to wrestle down durable answers. His writing can help to move discipleship from the dusty library of spiritual theory to the daily reality of our lives with Jesus.

Here's one last thing before we officially hit *Go*. I've known Preston for a couple of years. He lives this stuff in every way that matters: in his church, with his students and colleagues, with his friends, within his family, and in his soul.

Preston also grows an awesome beard and named his dog Tank. He's the real deal.

Following Jesus matters. I hope you use *Go* to bring discipleship into sharp focus, growing in your love for Christ and your joy in the journey *with others.*

Let's *Go!*

David Kinnaman
President, Barna Group
Ventura, California
May 2016

1

A HOMELESS PEASANT BORN IN A FEEDING TROUGH: THE SCANDAL OF FOLLOWING JESUS

HE WAS AN UNMARRIED peasant who was executed by the state for treason. Many of his friends were criminals, sinners, thugs, and misfits. Few of them were religious. He got kicked out of his home church (or synagogue) after saying things that deviated from the status quo. He spent most of his time with drunks, gluttons, fornicators, and thieves. He was so close to sinners that the religious leaders thought he was one. And nearly everything he said and did made religious people mad—such as when he told them to turn the other cheek, love their enemies, and give their money to the poor.

Jesus—the Jewish prophet-king from Nazareth—was dangerous. He wasn't tame. He wasn't predictable. He wasn't safe.

Even though he befriended immoral people, he upheld a

moral standard that was so impossible to obey that he walked out of a grave for us to attain it. He wasn't very sensitive to those seeking to follow him. He never eased anyone into the kingdom or said things that people wanted to hear. Jesus was a hard-hitting, enemy-loving, harlot-embracing, wild-eyed Messiah, who resisted doing things the way we've always done them. The biblical Jesus hits us between the eyes with truth and embraces us with tears when we disobey that truth. Jesus demanded that "if anyone would come after me"—that is, become a *disciple*—"let him deny himself and take up his cross daily and follow me" (Luke 9:23). As Dietrich Bonhoeffer used to say, "When Jesus calls a man, he bids him come and die."[1]

In this book we will explore what it means to become like Jesus, which means that it's a book about discipleship. When we talk about "becoming more like Jesus," we've got to slam our clichés on the operating table and dissect them to see if they're biblical. And this book is going to serve as the surgeon. When we talk about discipleship and becoming more Christlike, we've got to keep asking: *What does it mean to become like Jesus?*

The Moral Jesus of Therapeutic Deism

As we'll see, discipleship means becoming more like Jesus. This doesn't necessarily mean we should sell our homes and walk around the streets as homeless peasants. But I do think we need to take a fresh look at the scandalous nature of becoming Christlike.

If I can be completely honest, I've never had a huge desire to write a book about discipleship (don't tell my publisher).

I just figured that all the pastors and churches in America are doing a pretty good job. And if it ain't broke, why write a book about it?

But then I read the recent Barna study *The State of Discipleship*, and my desire to write this book was ignited.[2] In 2014, the international outreach ministry The Navigators commissioned the Barna Group, a Christian research firm, to perform an extensive survey of adult Christians, Christian scholars and influencers, and ministry and church leaders about their understanding and practice of discipleship. Some of the results of that study were informative; others were encouraging. But many of the results were depressing. We'll unpack some of the depressing details in due time, but to sum it up: The American church is not doing very well at discipling its people. Which is a big problem since discipleship means *becoming like Christ.*

The State of Discipleship revealed that our methods of making disciples are broken. Whatever we're doing, it's not working. Few churches and Christian leaders are effectively helping people become more like Jesus. Reading the results of that study really fired me up to want to write this book. Once I realized that our methods of making disciples have proved ineffective, I decided to peek behind the curtain to see what was going on.

One of the problems I found was that many Christians who are trying to become like Christ are not becoming like the Christ of the Bible—that radical Jewish peasant-prophet from Galilee. Instead, they are seeking to conform to the god of *moral therapeutic deism.* And when I peeked behind the curtain (that is, read the Barna study), my suspicions were confirmed.

Moral therapeutic deism is a phrase coined by sociologists Christian Smith and Melinda Lundquist Denton in their groundbreaking book *Soul Searching*.[3] Their study was focused on the religious beliefs of American teens, but it captures the typical beliefs of many American Christians:

- God exists and watches over the world.
- He wants us to be good people who are nice to others.
- The goal in life is to be happy and feel good about oneself.
- God isn't too involved in our lives unless we need him to solve a problem.
- Good people go to heaven when they die.

The God who exists in the minds of many churchgoers is "one who exists, created the world, and defines our general moral order, but not one who is particularly personally involved in one's affairs—especially affairs in which one would prefer not to have God involved."[4]

Of course, not every Christian thinks this way. But a surprising number do. My evidence for this used to be anecdotal—based on my own limited experience with other Christians. But then I read *The State of Discipleship* (and other studies like it), and my anecdotal experience was confirmed.

While many Christians say they want to become more like Jesus, the Jesus they're imagining is largely a modern (and American) religious and cultural construct. He's a Jesus who wants us to be good people, work an honest job, go to church as often as we can, be wise with our money, save up enough to retire well, raise well-behaved kids who don't drink or party or have sex before marriage, and be nice to our neighbors while seeking justice for our enemies. But the short-haired, dark-skinned, unmarried peasant who received the death penalty for treason—the Jesus of the Bible—neither modeled this nor taught it. If we're going to become like Jesus, we need to clear aside the clutter and see this Jesus for who he really is.

What Is Discipleship?

I've been a Christian for more than twenty years. This means I've heard the words *disciple, discipleship,* and *discipling* (a word unrecognized by Microsoft Word) at least 13 billion times. Like many Christian buzzwords, discipleship terms clutter the church airwaves, yet few people understand what they actually mean.

This could be bad news for a book about discipleship. We can't get very far until we clearly know what it is we're even talking about.

So what is discipleship? Is a disciple a special kind of Christian? Or one of the original twelve men who followed Jesus around in the first century? Can you be a disciple without being discipled by an older, more mature Christian? Is discipleship a program, a small group, a curriculum, a way of life, or something that only pastors and elders do? Are committed Christians disciples, while other less spiritual Christians are just plain old Christians?

The word *disciple* (Greek: *mathetes*) occurs at least 230 times in the Gospels and twenty-eight times in Acts.[5] According to the way it's used, *disciple* is simply another term for *Christian*. We see this most clearly in Acts 11:26: "In

HOW DO PEOPLE TALK ABOUT DISCIPLESHIP?

THE FOLLOWING ARE THE TERMS CHRISTIANS MOST PREFER FOR "DISCIPLESHIP"

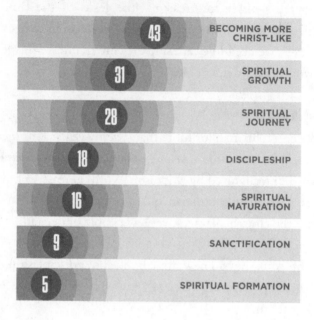

43	BECOMING MORE CHRIST-LIKE
31	SPIRITUAL GROWTH
28	SPIRITUAL JOURNEY
18	DISCIPLESHIP
16	SPIRITUAL MATURATION
9	SANCTIFICATION
5	SPIRITUAL FORMATION

Antioch the *disciples* were first called *Christians*" (emphasis added). Other passages (for example, Acts 4:32; 6:2, 7) use the term *disciple* simply to mean *believer*.

The terms *disciple* and *discipleship* aren't unique to the New Testament. Many people in the ancient world considered themselves to be disciples or disciplers. The great philosophers of Greece often referred to their pupils—their learners—as disciples. In its most basic sense, the word *disciple* simply means "a learner" or "one who is taught."

By New Testament times, the term *disciple* described one who was not just a learner but also devoted to a particular person, culture, or religion. Being a disciple meant being someone who followed and imitated the life and teaching of a great master. Discipleship was the process of learning from and becoming like that master. Plato was a disciple of Socrates, Zaleucus was a disciple of Pythagoras, and so on and so forth.

For some, "following" their master as a disciple might have been quite literal. The twelve disciples (also called *apostles*) named in the Gospels literally followed Jesus around in Israel. For others, being a follower of a master simply meant adhering to his teaching and seeking to imitate his life. The New Testament consistently uses the term *disciple* in this way: It describes all Christ followers, not some hyperspiritual subgroup who *really* takes this Jesus-freak thing seriously.

To be a disciple of Jesus, therefore, is to be a learner, an imitator, and a follower of Jesus. Discipleship is the process by which all Christians seek to become more like their Master. To be a Christian is to be a disciple, and every disciple—Christian—should seek to be like the Master.

According to *The State of Discipleship,* most Christians and Christian leaders agree—on paper—that "becoming more like Jesus" is fundamental to the Christian life. Yet on the whole, churches are not doing an effective job at making disciples who make disciples. Here are four pieces of evidence.

Christian Leaders Say "No"

According to the Barna study, only 1 percent of leaders say, "Churches are doing very well at discipling new and young believers." A sizable majority—six in ten (60 percent)—feels that churches are discipling "not too well." Contrast this with the responses of people outside of church leadership:

> Christian adults, however, have a very different perspective than their leaders: 52 percent of those who have attended church in the past six months say their church "definitely does a good job helping people grow spiritually" and another 40 percent say it "probably" does so.[6]

So leaders say churches are not doing a great job, and non-leaders generally say they are. What do we make of this disconnect?

For one, I don't think someone who has attended church "at least once in the last six months" will necessarily give the most accurate evaluation of the church's effectiveness. Someone who goes to the hospital a few times a year is probably not the best authority on whether the hospital is doing a good job. I'd rather ask the doctors and nurses who are there every day doing the work. I'm not saying we need to canonize the opinion of church leaders. But I do think their analysis is closer to the mark.

The Barna study also shows how many people are engaging in what the study calls "discipleship activities." "Despite believing that their church emphasizes spiritual growth, only 20 percent of Christian adults are involved in some sort of discipleship activity." These activities include "attending Sunday school or fellowship group, meeting with a spiritual mentor, studying the Bible with a group, or reading and discussing a Christian book with a group."[7] In other words, *The*

State of Discipleship reveals that a relatively low percentage of Christians are involved in church beyond attending (most) Sunday services.

But then again, just because someone is attending a church program doesn't guarantee that discipleship is happening. Some Bible studies are amazing avenues of spiritual growth. Others, though, are incubators for heresy, legalism, gossip, or cultic displays of power and control. I've been to some life-giving Sunday school classes. But I've also been bored to death by irrelevant and confusing monologues delivered—often read—by kindhearted but incessantly dull teachers. Or what if the college quarterback gets saved, starts leading a Bible study, and the attendance goes through the roof, especially among teenage girls? Are they wanting to grow closer to Jesus or closer to a guy with six-pack abs? God only knows. Certainly we can't evaluate the church's discipleship based merely on attendance figures.

Besides, what are discipleship activities anyway? Can we really determine whether people are "becoming more like Christ" based on their Sunday school and Bible study attendance? Did Jesus himself attend or put on any of these discipleship activities? Many churches today on the West Coast, where I'm from, don't even have Sunday school. The single mom who works on Tuesday nights will find it hard to get to the church's Bible study that meets on Tuesday nights. And what if I don't want to attend a Christian book discussion group? Does this mean I don't desire to "become like Christ?"

There's nothing inherently wrong with these activities. They can play a vital role in one's desire to become more like

When Jesus said "come follow me," he wasn't heading to Sunday school. He was on his way to heal the sick, befriend a tax collector, stand up for an adulteress, and proclaim good news to the poor.

Christ. But we can't determine whether a disciple is growing in Christ based on their attendance of church activities. Even if they are growing in their knowledge of Jesus through these activities, such learning should fuel their passion to live this stuff out. We must also do the work that Jesus calls disciples to *do*. Learning without doing is not really learning. We learn by doing, not just by learning alone. When Jesus said "come follow me," he wasn't heading to Sunday school. He was on his way to heal the sick, befriend a tax collector, stand up for an adulteress, and proclaim Good News to the poor.

Discipleship and mission go hand in hand. You can't have one without the other. And mission—impacting the community for Christ—is most effective outside the four walls of the church. We'll tease this out more thoroughly in chapter 7, so let's move on to the second piece of evidence that discipleship isn't working.

Millennials Say No

You may have heard that Millennials (people born after 1980) who were active in youth group are leaving the church in droves once they hit their twenties. According to David Kinnaman, "There is a 43 percent drop-off between the teen and early adult years in terms of church engagement."[8] According to Rainer Research, 70 percent of active youth group members leave the church by the time they're twenty-two years old.[9] Based on the current rate of departure, the Barna Group estimates that 80 percent of those raised in the church will be disengaged by the time they're twenty-nine years old.[10]

Some people yawn at statistics like these. "Young people have always been less likely to attend [church] than are older people," writes sociologist Rodney Stark.[11] When they grow up and have a few kids, they'll come back. They always do. No need to fret or change the way we do church.

But that's just it. They're not coming back. Even though eighteen- to thirty-five-year-olds often have the lowest rate of church attendance, the dropout rates themselves are higher than ever before. And eighteen- to thirty-five-year-olds today live their lives much differently than previous generations. Fewer are getting married; even fewer than that are having kids. These, traditionally, are the life events that drive people back to the church.[12] If we're waiting for them to settle down and return to church, we may be waiting for a while.

Not only that, but our Millennials are growing up in a world much different from previous generations.[13] The Internet alone has produced unparalleled shifts in how people live and think. Many sociologists have compared these changes to what took place after the invention of the printing press back in the fifteenth century. Just as information and literacy spread rapidly in the wake of the printing press, now information and power spread at the speed of light. We have little clue about the long-term social, mental, spiritual, relational, and civil impact this will bring. We stand right smack-dab in the center of the storm.

As we look at the trend of people leaving the church, we

shouldn't conclude that the sky is falling or that God's kingdom is coming to a screeching halt. Jesus promised that the gates of hell will not prevail against the church (Matthew 16:18). God is on the move! Still, as David Kinnaman says, "The dropout problem is, at its core . . . a disciple-making problem. The church is not adequately preparing the next generation to follow Christ faithfully in a rapidly changing culture."[14]

Some may say that people are leaving the church because they simply aren't Christians. And this is certainly true in some cases. Churches will always have people who attend for a season but then realize that they're not as much of a Jesus freak as they thought. The quarterback-turned-Bible-study-leader may put on thirty pounds; or he may leave the church, and his "followers" may follow him. But in many cases, people leave the church not because they had some beef with Jesus or were fly-by-night pseudo-Christians. "In fact, 51% of teens who leave the church in their twenties say they left because their spiritual needs were not being met."[15] At least 23 percent say that they actually wanted to know more about the Bible when they were in church but didn't get it.[16]

So they left. They left because *they didn't experience discipleship.* They left the church *to follow Jesus*—that wild-eyed, hard-hitting, homeless peasant who told the rich young ruler to give all of his stuff to the poor.

People shouldn't have to leave the church to find Jesus. But this is sometimes the case. Sociologists Josh Packard and Ashleigh Hope interviewed one hundred such "dechurched" folks—former lay leaders, active members, and congregants—for their book *Church Refugees.* Their study turned up surprising results.[17] They were expecting to find people who were burned out, overworked, or simply living on the sidelines of ministry. Instead, they found people who were still engaged, energetic, and desiring to make a difference in the world. Instead of being empowered by their churches in this desire, they were stiff-armed by bureaucracy or given a job that was restricted to Sunday services. As one dechurched Christian said: "There's nothing for me to do there [in church] that's meaningful."[18] Many dechurched leavers were bubbling over with passion and imagination about how they could tangibly share the love of Christ with their communities. Packard and Hope sum it up:

> The dechurched are leaving to do more, not less.
> The church isn't asking too much of people;
> it's asking the wrong things of them. . . . Jesus
> commanded his followers to care for the poor, the
> sick, and the hungry, [yet] the dechurched have
> experienced church as an organization that cares
> primarily for itself and its own members.[19]

Understanding Millennials and other dechurched Christians will be vital for our study. I'm going to make a case that many people would not leave the church if the church was doing a better, more holistic, and more creative job at discipling its people.

The Decline of Christians Says No

The exodus of Millennials from the church mirrors the overarching decline of Christianity in America. It's difficult to determine who's a Christian and who's not. Only God truly knows. But according to several studies, the number of genuine Christians is way lower than most people assume.

Some think that a large percentage of Americans are Christians. According to a Gallup survey, 45 percent of Americans claim to be born again.[20] Other research shows that 76 percent of Americans identify as Christian.[21] But claiming to be something and actually living it out are two different things. I remember talking to an Iraqi friend of mine about his faith. "I'm a Christian," he confessed. I got excited and probed a little deeper about his faith commitment. "Oh, I actually don't believe in God," he told me. For him, being a "Christian" was a cultural way of saying he wasn't Muslim.

Just because some people tick off the "Christian" box in a religious survey doesn't mean they've put their faith and hope in Jesus Christ. According to several independent surveys, the number of genuine Christians in America—who show some evidence of actually following Jesus—is around 8 percent.[22] According to George Barna, this percentage is down by about 30 percent since 1991. Pastor and author John Dickerson estimates that the percentage will be down to about 4 percent in the next thirty years if current trends continue. Reversing that trend is a discipleship concern.

Maybe you feel that your church or other churches in your city are growing. And maybe they are. But whenever churches grow, we have to ask where the growth came from and why it is occurring. That is, we have to distinguish between *transfer* growth and *conversion* growth. Conversion growth is when a church grows because people are getting saved and coming to church for the first time. Transfer growth is when people leave one local church to attend another. Transfer growth is not often the best way to measure whether discipleship is happening. It's not all bad, but it's not all good either. After all, Jesus never commanded his followers to "go into all nations and transfer Christians from one church to another."

If your church is growing because other people are leaving another church and coming to yours, then you still have to ask the discipleship question: What are those other churches not doing in discipling their people? And how will your growing church disciple these new members? Many newcomers stick around for a while but then move on after the new-church buzz wears off.

The Biblical Illiteracy Rate Says No

One of the most ironic facts in the church today is that access to the Bible is the highest it's ever been, yet so is biblical illiteracy. The average American (not just Christian) owns 4.4 Bibles. The number is even higher for Christians, and yet only 45 percent of those who regularly attend church read the Bible more than once a week, and almost 20 percent say they *never* read the Bible.[23] Despite owning several Bibles and having instant access to the Bible online and through smartphone apps, Christians don't appear to be opening it up very often.

And it shows. According to a Barna study, only 19 percent of people who identify as "born again" Christians have a Christian worldview (defined as holding to some basic tenets of the historic Christian faith).[24] For instance, 46 percent of born-again adults believe in absolute moral truth. Only 40 percent of Christians think that Satan is a "real force."

Most shocking are the percentages of Christians who strongly reject a works-based approach to salvation. Even though salvation by grace through faith alone is a basic truth in the New Testament, only 47 percent of born-again Christians strongly reject the notion that it's possible to work your way to heaven, and only 62 percent strongly believe that Jesus was sinless.[25] It's no wonder that 68 percent of Christians believe that the famous dictum "God helps those who helps themselves" is a verse in a Bible.[26] It's not. It actually comes close to a verse in the Qur'an.[27]

The lack of biblical literacy among Christians is again a discipleship problem. Don't get me wrong. I don't think we can reduce discipleship to a "worldview" curriculum. Discipleship is about transformation, not just transferring information. But there has to be at least some correlation between *right thinking* and *right living*. "Loving God with our mind" as Jesus commanded is certainly part of what it means to become "more like Jesus." Discipleship is more than just learning, but it's not less. Biblical illiteracy is a symptom of poor discipleship.

Where Do We Go from Here?

In the following pages, I'm going to interact with Barna's *The State of Discipleship* study and other studies that have analyzed Christian discipleship in the United States. I won't merely list a bunch of statistics, but I will examine the statistics and data to figure out what the church has been doing to disciple its people well and how the church can do a better job at making disciples who make disciples, who go on and—you guessed it—make disciples.

I will also interact with other relevant studies and authorities in addition to the Barna study:

- pastors and scholars who have been thinking and writing about discipleship;
- Christians and leaders who have thought through discipleship on a less public level;
- various books and studies on Millennials and the church; and
- personal friends, acquaintances, churchgoing Christians, and Christian "dropouts" whom I've met over the years.

My last source deserves some explanation. I've never been a full-time pastor, yet I've been heavily involved in church life as a deacon, elder, lay leader, teacher, or preacher in many different churches in my twenty-plus years as a Christian. I'm also a writer and a speaker, which means I get to visit and speak at many different churches around the United States (and the world). I've been exposed to the different ways in which Christians are "doing church" and discipling their people, which has been incredibly informative and eye-opening.

I used to think that not being a full-time pastor would disqualify me from writing a book on discipleship. But this way of thinking—that only pastors are qualified to talk about discipleship—is actually a big part of the problem. All Christians are disciples and disciplers. We all are missionaries and ministers who are called to serve God in his kingdom. But I'm getting ahead of myself. We'll unpack all of this in the following pages.

So here's a quick teaser of what's to come.

Chapter 2 will talk about *grace.* If we don't have a firm understanding of grace, our discipleship rocket will never get off the ground.

Chapter 3 shows why *relationships* are far more necessary than programs for discipleship. Programs aren't bad. But programs without relationships have proven ineffective in helping people become more like Christ.

Chapter 4 makes the claim—and some will dispute this, but trust me, it's biblical—that Christians can't adequately become more like Christ on their own. We need other people. We need *community.*

Chapter 5 tries to blow the doors off church so that our faith can permeate our entire lives, not just our Sunday mornings. Christian discipleship should be *holistic,* not compartmentalized.

Chapter 6 argues that *biblical literacy* among Christians is a serious discipleship issue. People are dropping like flies from the church, partly because Christians appear to have their heads buried in the sand—ignoring the tough intellectual issues of the day.

Chapter 7 reveals that biblical discipleship includes *mission,* not just morality. You can be porn-free, drug-free, sex-free, alcohol-free, and never even watch movies on Netflix—and you could still be a terrible disciple. Morality is good. But without mission, it's merely religion.

Chapter 8 exposes the fact that our churches are not very diverse, and this lack of *diversity* (in ethnicity, age, and socioeconomic status) is an unforeseen hindrance to discipleship.

Chapter 9 challenges the very *structure* of how we do

church. Many churches (not all) have inherited a way of doing church that's way too expensive and complicated. And this can be a massive roadblock on our journey of becoming more like the Son of God, who was born in a feeding trough.

The final chapter will talk through how to implement some of the changes I suggest in this book. Whether you're a pastor, a lay leader, or a Christian who's not in any formal leadership role, you're called to be a disciple who makes disciples. We all must *go*. For some, the call to *go* will launch them overseas or across the border. For most, however, *going* will involve staying because the mission is all around us. We must all follow Jesus in the marketplace and in the streets, in our neighborhoods and at our schools, through our relationships with both Christians and non-Christians. We are all called to *go*—and make disciples who make disciples.

So let's dive in and talk about that aggressive and scandalous and offensive thing called grace—God's stubborn delight in his enemies.

GOD'S SCANDALOUS DELIGHT: HOW GRACE MAKES US MORE LIKE JESUS

How are you doing spiritually?

No, really. I want you to answer the question. How are you doing spiritually? Take a few seconds and think about it. Don't worry. No one's watching. Just answer the question in your mind. It'll just be between you and God. And, well, God already knows how you're doing.

Rather than trying to guess what you said, let me share with you how I would respond to the question. When someone asks me how I'm doing spiritually, the first two things that come to mind are Bible reading and prayer. As a Bible professor, my Bible reading is usually pretty good, though I feel a bit guilty since it's part of my job. I often wonder how much Bible reading I would be doing if I were a mechanic or a business owner instead of a "professional" Christian. Most of my Bible reading these days has to do with preparing to teach a Bible class or researching the Scriptures for the latest book I'm writing. If I were a lawyer, a doctor, or a stay-at-home mom (I mean, dad), would I be reading the Bible as much as I am now? Or at all?

In terms of my prayer life, um . . . well . . . yeah, it pretty much stinks. On a good day I may spend some time in prayer in the morning—like, five to ten minutes. But those good days are few and far between. Usually I toss up a prayer here and there, often out of guilt that I don't pray as I should, or because I gave that Christianese knee-jerk reaction when a friend told me about a trial they were going through: "I'm sorry to hear that, brother. I'll pray for you." *Did I just say that? Did I mean it? Okay, I'd better pray for my friend right now because I don't want to be a liar.* Besides these guilt-driven prayers, it's not uncommon for me to go a few days and realize I haven't prayed at all.

By now, I usually have a softball-sized lump forming in my gut as I grow disgusted at how well, or not so well, I'm doing spiritually. And then I reflect on how I'm living.

My guilt is temporarily soothed by the fact that I'm generally living a pretty moral life. I'm not out getting drunk. I'm not having an affair. And if I can be completely honest, I haven't struggled with porn ever since I became a Christian. (Part of this is because I got saved in 1999, just before the Internet became an omnipresent beast, so I never had to wean myself off Internet porn. In my teen years, you had to actually buy a magazine or a VHS tape—remember those?)

I've got a healthy marriage and four wonderful kids.

I usually read the Bible to them at night, though we certainly go through seasons where my wife and I rush them off to bed so that we can squeeze in an extra hour of Netflix. Oh no. I forgot. *Netflix.* Maybe I'd be doing better spiritually if I didn't watch Netflix every single night of the week. Maybe I should read a book instead. Or maybe I should pray.

As I feel the weight of spiritual depression setting in, I remind myself that I love God's mission. Every year I take a mission trip to Nepal and serve the impoverished believers in that developing country. I give food to lepers. I preach the gospel to blind people. I teach the Scriptures to new and old believers. I absolutely love to experience God through these marginalized Christians living in the midst of a Hindu nation!

I don't leave my love for missions in Nepal. There's not a day that goes by when my heart isn't heavy for people who have been neglected by society, oppressed by the majority, or even shunned by the church. The other day, my family and I visited an international church that was filled with immigrants and refugees from Africa. The two-and-a-half-hour service was translated into Swahili. I was bubbling over with empathy as I talked with joy-filled believers who came to America to escape civil war and genocide. We worshiped Jesus together through several languages. It was epic.

Okay, so my Bible reading is going okay, depending on how you measure it. My prayer life is in need of some serious improvement. I really should do something about my Netflix addiction. (Maybe after I finish the last season of *The Walking Dead.*) I'm a decent husband and father, though I still have much room to grow. I truly love people, especially the marginalized. So how did I score? I don't know, maybe a 6 out of 10? Perhaps a 7? I guess it depends on how many points we get for prayer—or lack thereof. Maybe I scored more like a 5.

Do you see anything wrong with all of this? What's the common theme across everything I've said? You can see it quite easily by looking at a few key words; they occur in almost every sentence that I've written above.

I. Me. My.

I've reduced my entire "spiritual life" to my fragile pursuit of God. I never even factored in *God's relentless pursuit of me.*

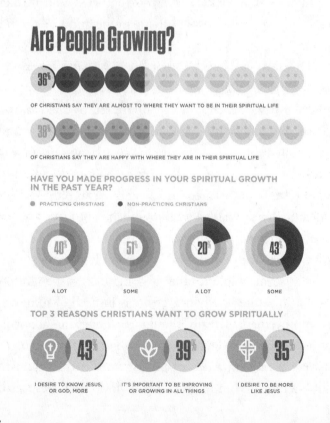

Are People Growing?

36% OF CHRISTIANS SAY THEY ARE ALMOST TO WHERE THEY WANT TO BE IN THEIR SPIRITUAL LIFE

38% OF CHRISTIANS SAY THEY ARE HAPPY WITH WHERE THEY ARE IN THEIR SPIRITUAL LIFE

HAVE YOU MADE PROGRESS IN YOUR SPIRITUAL GROWTH IN THE PAST YEAR?

● PRACTICING CHRISTIANS ● NON-PRACTICING CHRISTIANS

| 40% | 51% | 20% | 43% |
| A LOT | SOME | A LOT | SOME |

TOP 3 REASONS CHRISTIANS WANT TO GROW SPIRITUALLY

| 43% | 39% | 35% |
| I DESIRE TO KNOW JESUS, OR GOD, MORE | IT'S IMPORTANT TO BE IMPROVING OR GROWING IN ALL THINGS | I DESIRE TO BE MORE LIKE JESUS |

Have you ever considered that when we fail to read the Bible and listen to God, God never stops listening to us? When we forget to talk to God through prayer, God never stops talking to us. When we don't love our spouses and kids and neighbors and enemies the way we ought, God never stops loving us. Even when we look at porn or delight in too much Netflix, God never stops delighting in us.

God doesn't delight in our sin. But he delights in us *even though* we sin. God's love isn't based on what we do or don't do. It's based on who God is and what Christ has done for us. His love doesn't fluctuate when we perform well or not so well. His love is an outflow of who he is: a God who loved us "while we were still sinners" (Romans 5:8).

It's fruitless to talk about discipleship without first talking about grace. Grace is the foundation and structure of discipleship. By grace God creates disciples. By grace God cultivates disciples. And it's by God's grace that we are transformed into Christlikeness. Grace enables us to be like Jesus, forgives us when we fail to act like Jesus, and empowers us to cling to Jesus in the midst of our brokenness. Jesus, not you or I, is the center of discipleship. In the words of Eugene Peterson, "Discipleship is a process of paying more and more attention to God's righteousness and less and less attention to our own."[1]

Let me be clear. I believe that Bible reading, prayer, purity, and many other things we do—or shouldn't do—are important. Discipleship includes our obedience, our pursuit of God. Spiritual disciplines and personal morality play a *vital* role in our effort to become like Christ.

It's fruitless to talk about discipleship without first talking about grace.

I don't subscribe to a version of Christianity that believes we should "let go and let God"—just lounging around in our PJs, waiting for God to act. But the Scriptures are clear that grace must be the centerpiece of discipleship. Without a rich understanding of grace, our efforts to become like Christ will fail. Without an authentic reliance on God's unmerited delight, we cannot follow the sinless Savior. Unless God stubbornly pursues us—which he does—we simply can't pursue him.

In his excellent book *Gospel-Centered Discipleship*, Jonathan Dodson rightly stresses the relationship between grace and discipleship:

> The wonderful news of the gospel is that Jesus frees us from trying to impress God or others because he has impressed God on our behalf. . . . Gospel-centered discipleship is not about how we perform but who we are—*imperfect people, clinging to a perfect Christ, being perfected by the Spirit.*[2]

Discipleship is not about impressing God or others, and it's not about performing well. Discipleship is primarily about Jesus and his continual work in us through the Holy Spirit.

Let's ask our opening question again and answer it with the Good News of Jesus. Rather than asking, "How well are you doing spiritually?" let's put it differently: *How is God making you more like Christ?*

I'm on an imperfect journey of becoming like Christ. When I was a sinner, the Father set his affection on me and sent his Son to die for me. Even though I wasn't delightful,

God delighted in me; even though I was running from God, God was running to me—and he's faster than I am.

God looks upon me as a beautiful work of art, even though I have so much ugliness in my life. I often feel value-less, but God paid the highest price to purchase me. I am prized and honored in the eyes of my Creator.

I am redeemed, forgiven, adopted, and beloved. I am known, pursued, and the object of God's infinite *affection*. When I'm apathetic toward God, he's never apathetic toward me. Though I'm prone to wander, he's prone to pursue. I am the crown, the jewel, the apex of God's majestic creation.

And I am never alone. My Savior is with me even to the end of the age. He's with me because he *wants to be with me*. When I sin, God forgives. When I fail, Christ succeeds. Though I have no strength to obey, God strengthens me through his Holy Spirit who lives in me.

> My old self has been crucified with Christ. It is no longer I who live, but Christ lives in me. So I live in this earthly body by trusting in the Son of God, who loved me and gave himself for me.
>
> GALATIANS 2:20, NLT

> God is working in me, giving me the desire and the power to do what pleases him.
>
> PHILIPPIANS 2:13, NLT[3]

Father. Son. Holy Spirit. Our spiritual lives are cradled and enabled by his powerful presence.

Performance-Based Discipleship

Most Christians don't think of their spiritual lives like this. Again, 68 percent of born-again Christians think that the expression "God helps those who help themselves" comes from the mouth of God. And it shows. According to another Barna study, three out of five churchgoing Christians "equate Christianity with a list of moral rules to be followed." That is roughly the same percentage as unchurched people.[4]

Another recent study looked at whether churchgoing Christians more resemble the attitudes and actions of Christ or the Pharisees.[5] Christians were asked questions such as the following:

- Do you regularly choose to have meals with people with very different faith or morals from yourself?
- Do you see God-given value in every person, regardless of their past or present condition?
- Do you feel compassion for people who are not following God and are doing immoral things?

You know, the things Jesus thought and did on a regular basis. The survey also asked questions that reflect the attitudes and actions of the Pharisees:

- Do you tell others that the most important thing in my life is following God's rules?
- Do you think that people who follow God's rules are better than those who do not?
- Do you believe that it's not your responsibility to help people who won't help themselves?

The results were quite disappointing. Fifty-one percent of self-identified Christians are primarily pharisaical in attitude and action. Only 14 percent tended to be Christlike in attitude and action.

To be sure, surveys and statistics aren't inerrant. They can't give us a perfect window into the heart of every person. But I do believe they can give us a decent ballpark view of how people actually think and act. As I reflect on the different Christians I've interacted with over the years, the results of this survey aren't too shocking. Christians often talk about grace and say they've been saved by grace alone. But when you dig into how they live, they appear to rely much more on their own performance than on Christ's finished work on the cross. And they project this performance-driven version of the gospel onto others, then back onto themselves. And down we tumble down the rabbit hole of legalism. At the bottom lie piles of Christians who are trying to become moral without clinging to and celebrating the finished work of Christ.

One of the reasons our discipleship is failing is that we've left the gospel out of it. Intuitively, many Christians think that the gospel saves us but has little ongoing relevance for our discipleship. But discipleship, or becoming more like Christ, is all about diving deeper and deeper into his unconditional favor for us. You cannot become more like Christ and not become more and more addicted to his grace. I love how Jonathan Dodson puts it:

It is continual trust in his death and life for my sin and righteousness that matures me, drawing me deeper and deeper into an ever-present hope of acceptance before God. This hope is Jesus Christ as my Lord and Redeemer, not a better moral track record. When we absorb the radical gospel focus of the Gospel Commission, it compels the mission of making disciples who, in turn, preach and teach the gospel of grace to others.[6]

Or more succinctly: "The gospel that makes disciples is the very same gospel that matures disciples."[7]

The Condemnation of Performing

The apostle Paul looked at his performance and cringed. He had given in. His renewed resolve and good intentions failed. He heard his performance yelling out his identity: "wretch" (Romans 7:15-24).

We use other words today when our performance pastes an identity on us. Loser. Failure. Fake. Different words but the same dilemma—we can never perform our way out of condemnation. The good news of the gospel is this: Our identity is now based not on our performance but on the performance of Jesus. It is grace alone that changes the wretch into a saint.

BILL TELL, national staff development specialist, The Navigators; author of *Lay It Down*

Countercultural

We live in a country that's obsessed with performance. From the time we are kids, we try to outperform our classmates in school or our fellow athletes on the field. If we're going to make the all-star team, we must perform better than the rest. If we want to get a girlfriend or boyfriend, we have to look better than the competition. And we never outgrow our performance-driven culture. We advance in life by performing well in college. We'll get a raise at our jobs if we perform well. We'll have a better chance at getting married if we can make ourselves look better than we are. Your Facebook "you" is much prettier, much happier, and has many more friends than the real "you." Our entire lives are shaped by performance and by making a good impression.

Enter Jesus: "Come to me, all of you who are weary from performance, and I will give you rest" (Matthew 11:28, author's rendering). Our performance comes to a screeching halt when we meet Jesus. He's not impressed with our moral track record, and he yawns at our laundry list of sins. He meets us where we are and walks with us through thick and thin.

Just think of how Jesus rolled with his first disciples. Peter is a prime example of a disciple whose spiritual walk was upheld by grace. Quick to speak and slow to think, Peter's fragile character makes my sad prayer life look a little less embarrassing. On one occasion, he tells Jesus that he won't let him get crucified. Jesus rebukes him: "Get behind me, Satan!" (Matthew 16:23). Wow! Have you been accused of speaking the very words of Satan? Peter has. He was accused by Jesus himself.

On the night Jesus was betrayed, he washed his disciples' feet. Peter tried to stop him, but then Jesus told him that if he didn't let Jesus wash his feet, Peter would "have no share with" Jesus (John 13:8). Peter's response is a bit uncomfortable:

"Lord, not my feet only but also my hands and my head!" (John 13:9). Give me a sponge bath, Jesus! Talk about awkward. And what about that time when Peter denied Jesus three times (Matthew 26:69-75)? This is truly unbelievable and encouraging all at the same time. Peter has been hanging out with Jesus for three years. When asked whether he is a follower of Jesus, Peter says that he doesn't even know the guy.

"Hey, weren't you hanging out with this man from Nazareth?"

"No sir, I wasn't. I don't even know the man."

Imagine if your pastor got up next Sunday and told the entire congregation: "I don't even know who Jesus is." He'd be fired on the spot and rushed out of church. But Jesus is far less threatened. He's less threatened by our doubts than we are. He knows how fragile our faith actually is—even if we try to spackle over our weakness with good Christian performance. Just before Peter denied Jesus, Jesus told him that he would never let him go: "Simon, Simon, Satan has asked to sift each of you like wheat. But I have pleaded in prayer for you, Simon, that your faith should not fail" (Luke 22:31-32, NLT).

Peter's faith was created and upheld by Jesus himself. Were it not for Christ, Peter would have continued to deny that he knew Jesus. Like that old hymn "Come Thou Fount":

> Let thy goodness like a fetter bind my wandering
> heart to thee.
> Prone to wander—Lord, I feel it—prone to leave
> the God I love.
> Here's my heart, O take and seal it, seal it for thy
> courts above.

Peter is a perfect example of what discipleship looks like. We are zealous yet apathetic, full of faith and doubt, obedient one day and disobedient the next. We are on an imperfect journey toward a perfect Savior who upholds us by his grace and promises to never let us go. We all, like Peter, are prone to wander, prone to leave the God we love. But God's goodness binds our wandering hearts to him. Discipleship will never get off the ground until we cling to this basic point.

Being Discipled in Grace

So far, we've explored grace from 30,000 feet. It's easy to say *the same grace that saves us also matures us*, but what does this look like? Here are four ways that grace-based discipleship can help us become more like Jesus.

Freedom to live authentically. I've got to be honest, it was really hard to share my sketchy prayer life in this chapter. I mean seriously, it's now in print! Forever. For all to see. There was something brewing inside me that wanted to keep it to myself. Every line I wrote about my prayer life was incredibly difficult. Why?

Performance. Pride. A desire to impress other people. Fear of the shame of spiritual failure.

We all have it in us. We're scared to admit where we're not "performing" well. But discipleship is all about confessing our failures and inviting God (and others) to redeem these failures. I can never improve my prayer life unless I admit that there's much to improve on. We become more like Jesus only after we admit that we're nothing like Jesus. We shouldn't delight in our failures, but we need to admit them.

Once we're real about where we're at, we can rely on God to take us where he wants us to be.

Christians, and especially those of us who are leaders, need to cultivate environments where people feel free to be authentic. Jesus is not glorified when we try to make ourselves look better than we are. We don't want people to stay where they are—discipleship is about moving from who we are to who Jesus wants us to be. But there's no point in creating church environments where people feel pressured to appear further along than they actually are.

David Kinnaman shares some troubling statistics in his book *You Lost Me*. In a survey of Millennials who have a Christian background, many reported feeling that church isn't a safe place to wrestle with tough questions or admit doubts about God. More than a third said that they didn't feel safe asking their most pressing life questions in church. One in five said they have had a crisis in life that has made them doubt their faith. One in ten said that they aren't allowed to talk about their doubts in church.[8]

Churches that aren't safe places for people to express doubt will have a hard time discipling people. After all, Abraham, David, Elijah, Peter, Thomas, and even John the Baptist would have had a really tough time fitting in at a church that didn't allow for doubt. After all, our biblical heroes of the faith *doubted*. Yet they're still heroes.

A performance-based church environment will prevent disciples from genuinely wrestling with the deep issues of life—the things that cause them to doubt. But a grace-based environment will liberate disciples to invite others to address their deepest and darkest struggles head-on.

Freedom from people-pleasing. Performance-based disciple-ship feeds off of human approval. I know this from experi-ence, and you probably do as well. Think about those days when you are spiritually off the charts. You wake up early and pray for an hour. You read the Bible for another hour. You fast all day, witness to a coworker, and cancel your Netflix subscription (for now). You are really pursuing God!

Aren't you just dying to let other Christians know about it? When your pastor asks how your day was, doesn't it feel so good sharing all the details? "I'd love to meet for lunch, pastor, but see, I'm actually fasting today. Plus, I'm going out to lunch with this coworker that I've been witnessing to . . ." When we're performing well, we're often eager to let others know about it.

A good friend of mine just burned out on ministry. He was a pastor at a thriving church, and he was doing many amazing things to further God's kingdom. He was teaching, preaching, counseling, and serving. He was working very hard—and that was part of the problem. He just couldn't say no—to anything. He just kept doing, doing, doing. He was performing well for Christ. Or at least he thought he was. Actually, he was performing himself into exhaustion to please others. His hyperactive, nonstop, 24/7 performance for Christ was actually crushing him. He nearly destroyed his family and spent a whole month in counseling because his performance wasn't driven by grace but by a desire to look good in front of people.

Our culture admires the hard worker. We elevate the one who produces more than the rest. There's a spark of virtue in the drive to excel and succeed, but it's only a blink away from falling prey to legalistic performance and self-serving workaholism.

Trying to perform well for other humans will stifle our quest to become more like Christ. Engaging in spiritual disciplines such as Bible reading, fasting, and prayer are all very valuable and even necessary for our discipleship. But when we engage in them as ways to make ourselves look spiritual in the eyes of people, these disciplines actually work against our spirituality (see Matthew 6:1-5).

Since all Christians are deeply shaped by our performance-driven culture, we will need to work extra hard—reminding people *daily* that the gospel liberates us from trying to impress other people with our spirituality. Pharisaical pressure from other Christians needs to be confronted as aggressively as blatant immorality. Any Christian—especially a Christian leader—who makes others feel unspiritual or unmotivated to admit their failures is a roadblock to discipleship.

God knows how broken and messed up we really are. Yet he's still pleased with us because he was pleased with Jesus. We need to make much of Christ's performance, rather than our own.

Grace-based accountability. Accountability groups can be a vital means of cultivating discipleship. According to *The State of Discipleship,* "*Accountability* is essential for busy, scattered people to make the time to invest in their spiritual growth."[9] It's tough to become more like Christ if other believers are not coming alongside you to keep you accountable.

However, accountability groups can also discourage people from becoming more like Jesus, especially if they are performance based rather than grace based. I love what

Jonathan Dodson says: "Although accountable relationships start with a noble aim—commitment to confession, encouragement, and prayer for one another—they often devolve into relationships based on rule keeping or rule breaking."[10] What often ends up happening is that people tend to put more faith in accountability than they do in the gospel. "The unfortunate result is a kind of legalism in which peer-prescribed punishments are substitutes for repentance and faith in Jesus."[11]

Churches should cultivate accountability relationships that seek to magnify the gospel. Christian accountability should never shame someone into obedience or make them feel unloved by God. True accountability should always celebrate God's finished work on the cross and his vast sea of forgiveness available to those who mess up.

Motivation to obey. The apostle Paul was criticized for giving people a license to sin by emphasizing grace too much. "And some people even slander us by claiming that we say, 'The more we sin, the better it is!'" (Romans 3:8, NLT). A few chapters later, Paul addressed this criticism head-on: "Should we keep on sinning so that God can show us more and more of his wonderful grace? Of course not!" (Romans 6:1-2, NLT). Grace doesn't cause people to sin, and it should never be a motivation to keep on sinning. A person who sins because of God's unconditional grace hasn't truly understood God's unconditional grace.

God's grace meets us where we are, but it doesn't leave us where we are. The same grace that encounters sinners also conquers sin. This is why Paul spends the first five chapters of Romans exploring God's unmerited favor and then spends the next three encouraging Christians toward obedience. Obedience flows from grace. True grace enables and produces obedience. I love how Paul puts it in 1 Corinthians 15:10: "But whatever I am now, it is all because God poured out his special favor on me—and not without results" (NLT).

Grace is not a cul-de-sac but a highway; it's not an off-ramp but an on-ramp toward obedience. This is why Paul says that grace is "not without results." He goes on to say that it was God's grace that caused him to work "harder than any of [the other apostles]." How? Because God's grace didn't putter out after saving Paul. It kept chipping away at Paul until it pushed obedience out the other side.

Grace and obedience aren't enemies. They're friends. Grace doesn't prevent obedience. Grace enables it. "Work out your own salvation," Paul says, "with fear and trembling." Sound legalistic? I know—it does to me, too. This is why Paul goes on to say, "For it is God who works in you, both to will and to work for his good pleasure" (Philippians 2:12-13). Work hard—by God's grace.

Grace and obedience aren't enemies. They're friends. Grace doesn't prevent obedience. Grace enables it.

Both obedience and grace should hang in the air of our discipleship communities. As we seek to become more like Christ, we should talk more and more about grace, not less. Grace doesn't just save us; it also sanctifies us. "No disciple will ever graduate from the school of grace," Dodson says. "We are born in grace and we breathe by grace."[12]

Whether your discipleship community consists of one-on-ones, triads, small groups, or large groups, the group's fuel tank must be filled with grace. When—not if—people fail, they need to be reassured that God is still for them, that he still scandalously delights in them, that their failures have been covered by the blood of Christ. Grace doesn't just get us in the door of salvation; it's what makes us more like Jesus.

People will never be able to obey God until they first believe they are accepted by God. Acceptance precedes obedience.

- - - - -

Grace-based discipleship frees us up to engage in meaning-ful and authentic relationships. And discipleship is all about relationships. When two (or three, or four) broken people come together and have nothing to hide, no one to impress, and no plastic image that they're trying to put on, it becomes so much easier to engage in honest relationships. And hon-est relationships are at the core of effective discipleship—the topic of our next chapter.

3

YOU CAN'T BECOME LIKE JESUS ALONE: AUTHENTIC RELATIONSHIPS IN DISCIPLESHIP

I'M NOT A VERY RELATIONAL PERSON. You might not believe this if you met me. I can turn on the friendliness when I need to, and I know how to ask questions and get to know people. In other words, I can fake it pretty well. But I actually like to be alone. Maybe love would be a better term—I *love* to be alone. I could be alone all week. Even two weeks straight, and it wouldn't bother me one bit. As long as I have a good book to read, a project to work on, good movies to watch, and a refrigerator packed full of meat, I'll be just fine.

That is why this chapter is tough to write, because I'm part of the problem. I'm the one that needs this chapter the most. You might need it too, but I *know* I need it. Because here's the thing: discipleship can't happen without relationships. Deep relationships. Authentic relationships. Relationships where people can share their intimate struggles, confess their socially unacceptable sins, and rely on others for spiritual strength.

But these types of relationships are fairly rare among Christians. Many Christians I talk to say they feel alone, unconnected, or isolated at church. They have some superficial friends, maybe one or two close friends if they're lucky. But on the whole, most Christians never get below the surface with their church communities.

Until we figure out how to cultivate deep relationships among Christians, our discipleship will continue to suffer.

One reason discipleship has suffered is that we have focused too heavily on discipleship programs rather than investing in authentic relationships. David Kinnaman sums up the problem:

> We are at a critical point in the life of the North American church; the Christian community must rethink our efforts to make disciples. Many of the assumptions on which we have built our work with young people are rooted in modern, mechanistic, and mass production paradigms. Some (though not all) ministries have taken cues from the assembly line, doing everything possible to streamline the manufacture of shiny new Jesus-followers, fresh from the factory floor. But disciples cannot be mass-produced. Disciples are handmade, one relationship at a time.[1]

Both *The State of Discipleship* and prominent discipleship leaders echo Kinnaman's plea.[2] If we are going to do a better job at discipleship, we can't rely on programs alone. We must foster authentic relationships as the means of transforming people into Christlikeness.

Discipleship should be a way of life, a holistic integration of the gospel into every fiber of our week. *The State of Discipleship* shows that this is especially true of Millennials who crave intimate relationships. Millennials value intimate relationships far more than Gen-Xers (my generation) and Boomers.

"MY FRIENDS HAVE BEEN VERY HELPFUL TO MY SPIRITUAL GROWTH."

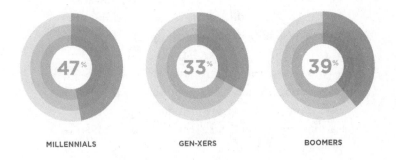

MILLENNIALS   GEN-XERS   BOOMERS

While this includes peer relationships, many Millennials desire intergenerational relationships from older believers as well.[3] *The State of Discipleship* shows that 59 percent of Millennials who remain active in their faith had a close relationship with an adult believer in their church (apart from their parents or pastor). Twenty-eight percent say that they were mentored by an older believer in church, while only

11 percent of those who dropped out of church said the same.[4] This shows that Millennials are much more likely to stay engaged in the faith if they are connected with older believers.

And it's not just Millennials. All Christians need to be in relationship with other believers if they desire to become more like Christ. Every single discipleship leader I've talked to (or whose books I've read) says the same thing: *Discipleship cannot happen apart from relationships.* You can have all kinds of killer programs, but if these programs don't also foster relationships, then growth toward Christlikeness will be minimal.

Iron Sharpening Iron

Discipleship is knowing and becoming like Christ—living in vibrant, fruitful relationship with him. What we do (personally or with others) is to be a means, not the end. Even disciple making can become a project or activity in and of itself rather than a privileged participation in the work of the Lord.

God uses friendships to bring an "iron sharpening iron" effect. Small-group Bible studies and discussion groups provide the opportunity for peer learning, motivation and encouragement. Pairs, trios, or groups meeting for prayer often open the door to experience God through others and to grow in faith. The strength of programs and systems is revealed in a relational context—providing a beginning point and concrete steps within the relationship toward a greater end: knowing Christ and making him known, and helping others do the same.

LINDY BLACK, associate US director, The Navigators

Rich relationships are also one of the main reasons why people stay connected to church and to Jesus.[5] Leaving a church is easy when you're not connected with other people. It's hard to leave if you are connected. Many Christians stay at a church because they are relationally connected, even if they don't love the teaching or worship or color of the carpets. Relationships—the deep ones, not the exhausting superficial ones—are often the glue that keeps us connected to our church communities.

A friend of mine recently left his church in search of another church that had better teaching and a more missional mind-set. He spent a few months at a church known for having some of the best teaching in town. But three months later, he returned to his old church. I asked him why, and he said, "I just had too many deep relationships with people at my home church. I couldn't stay away."

We shouldn't foster rich relationships, however, just to keep people in church. Otherwise, we become nothing more than an intimate country club. We should pursue relationships because it's part of what it means to become more like Jesus, and we can't pursue this impossible journey without a deep connection to others on the same journey.

A God So Near

In spite of the benefits of programs and large gatherings, discipleship at its core is relational. We see this throughout the Bible, beginning in the Garden of Eden, where God recognized that "it is not good for the man to be alone." Adam got pretty stoked when he saw Eve. So the two became one flesh and "knew" each other (Genesis 2:18-25). Adam's new companion became his wife, of course, but she also became a necessary figure to form a human *community.* Even if Adam and Eve never hooked up and got married, Adam's loneliness would have been solved, since he now had a fellow human to relate to.

God didn't just create Eve to be a wife; he created her because he knew that Adam couldn't live out his humanity in isolation.

You might find this shocking, but God didn't create marriage to solve our loneliness.[6] God created other humans to fill the void. Whenever marriage is described in Scripture, it's never viewed as a solution to loneliness.[7] In fact, when people find rich, satisfying relationships, it's usually with other believers of the same gender.[8] Singleness doesn't have to lead to loneliness.

Discipleship at its core is relational.

God created us—all of us—to be relational beings because God himself is relational. God doesn't exist as only one person, but as three persons in one. The Father, the Son, and the Holy Spirit live in eternal relationship with each other. And in order to invite us into that Trinitarian dance, the Father sent the Son to take on human flesh and walk among us. God didn't just want to relate to us from a distance. He didn't want to text us from heaven or tweet us once in a while to see how we're doing. He wanted to know us, relate to us, experience life with us. And this is why Jesus was born in a feeding trough—to show us just how far God was willing to go in order to be near to us.

Our God is a relational God. Since we are created in his image, we are relational people. If I'm truly honest with myself, my desire to be alone is often driven by sin and self-ishness. When I'm alone I can do what I want, when I want, and how I want to do it. I don't think about, let alone worry about, other people around me. I don't have to talk if I don't want to talk. I don't have to ask questions or show interest in someone else's life. I can just take care of myself.

Sounds pretty selfish. And sinful. In order for us to flourish as humans and become more like Christ, we must engage in intimate, sacrificial, authentic, non-superficial relationships.

Relational Discipleship in the Life of Jesus

When Jesus gathered his disciples, he called them into a relationship: "Come follow me." Even though he spoke to large crowds on occasion—sometimes it was unavoidable—the primary way in which he "discipled" his followers was through relationships. On the road, over a meal, on a boat under the hot Galilean sun. Discipleship wasn't something Jesus did in addition to his otherwise busy ministry week. Discipleship was the natural outgrowth of doing life with other people.

Most of the time, we see Jesus interacting with a small group of disciples. Usually it was the twelve apostles, though sometimes he singled out Peter, James, and John. But there were also Mary and Martha (Luke 10:38-42), Nicodemus (John 3:1-15), Zacchaeus (Luke 19:1-10), the unnamed woman at the well (John 4:1-26), Levi and his shady friends (Luke 5:27-32), and many other relational encounters recorded in the Gospels. These were not just random conversations but relational encounters, where Jesus was revealing himself and teaching people about what it means to follow him.

Jesus's primary mode of discipleship is relational, which is simply a continuation of God's desire to relate to us through the incarnation of Christ. On a few occasions we see Jesus teaching in larger settings: the Sermon on the Mount (Matthew 5–7), his speeches in the Temple (Matthew 23:1-36; John 7:28-39), and his parable-laced sermon by the sea (Matthew 13:1-25). Some of these, however, happened spontaneously as Jesus was hanging out and relating with his disciples (see Matthew 4:25–5:1). If we were to stand back and look at the life of Jesus as a whole, the bulk of his time was spent investing deeply in a few rather than addressing large groups of people.[9]

What's most shocking, though, is not *that* he engaged in relational discipleship, but *whom* he engaged with.

Whom Did Jesus Disciple?

I'll never forget talking to a fellow college professor about investing in the lives of students. I had just been hired at a fairly large Christian university. I didn't want to just spout off information in a classroom; I wanted to "disciple" my students. My classes had anywhere from forty to 150 students— and I was teaching a lot of classes! "How do you do it?" I asked my friend. "How do you know whom to invest in? Do you just focus on the ones with the most potential?"

I thought I was stating a no-brainer. When I was a baseball player, the coach would always take more time to invest in the most talented players, the ones who had a future. This is just good leadership, right? Wouldn't it be most efficient for me to single out the students who were the most godly, the most wise, the most hardworking—those who had the greatest potential?

My friend was always good at leading me to the right answer rather than spoon-feeding it to me. He responded, "That may be efficient and effective—but is it the most *Christian?*" As I mentally scanned the life of Christ, it hit me like a ton of Bibles: Jesus didn't single out the most promising, the best leaders, the naturally gifted and godly people. He actually singled out *the worst.*

Peter, as we saw in the last chapter, was a bumbling coward who never seemed to get it. I'm pretty sure Jesus considered him to be high-maintenance. I know I would. The other members of the "inner three," James and John, were a couple of hotheads whom Jesus should have sent to an anger management seminar rather than into the world to preach the gospel of love (see Luke 9:51-56). These two thugs would have made fine candidates for ISIS or maybe an inner-city gang. But instead, Jesus trained them to love their enemies and turn the other cheek.

Simon the Zealot and Matthew the tax collector were a fascinating pair. I'm not sure what Jesus was thinking when he brought these two together. Simon was probably a member of a feisty group of Jewish militants looking to overthrow the Roman occupation of Israel. Matthew was a Jewish sellout, a traitor who went to work for Rome in taking money from the hands of his hardworking Jewish neighbors. Simon and Matthew: You could not find a more contradictory pair!

Thomas was a cynic (John 11:16). Nathanael was sarcastic (John 1:46). And Judas, of course, would betray Jesus just after Jesus had washed his feet (John 13). If there were any kingdom-of-God-planting manuals in the first century, they surely would have advised Jesus *not* to select these twelve hoodlums. They're not going to get along. They're going to hinder your mission. *They're not worth your investment.*

But Jesus came to establish an upside-down kingdom, where enemies are loved and persecutors are prayed for. And he deliberately invested in the "foolish things of the world" to show off the wisdom of God (1 Corinthians 1:26-31, NIV). The Christian way is the countercultural way. And how much more powerful is it to see those whom the world considers unworthy go out and turn the world upside down (Acts 17:6)?

I'll never forget first meeting my friend Joseph Madison. I was leading a small group, and Joseph was a participant. Joseph was in his midsixties, single (never married), and, well . . . let's just say he wasn't the quarterback of the football team. The world would look at Joseph and say, "You have nothing to offer."

At first, it was tough to lead the group when Joseph was around. He seemed to talk too much and chime in with irrelevant information. He'd get flustered at our conversations or talk loudly over other people. I remember talking to a member of the group who had known Joseph for years. It turned out that Joseph had actually been a catalyst in restoring half a dozen marriages. "You wouldn't believe it!" my friend told me. "I don't know how he did it. He just dove into some broken relationships and became an agent of healing. If it wasn't for Joseph, those couples would have gotten a divorce."

I grew to love Joseph Madison. It was evident that he had a tender heart toward God and deeply cared for other people.

No one would have guessed that Joseph had the potential to become a "marriage counselor." And here's the thing: No program-driven church would ever let Joseph near a stage to give a marriage seminar. The stage is for good-looking professionals—not for sixty-year-old single people.

Maybe this is why Jesus didn't use the stage to turn the world upside down. He used the broken and busted, the marginalized and outcasts. He used and still uses people like Joseph Madison.

Four Ingredients of Relational Discipleship

Whether you're meeting one on one or in a small group, there are at least four ingredients that go into healthy relationships.

First, as we've seen before, *relationships must be authentic.* Honesty and depth may not happen overnight, but they must happen for discipleship to take place. This requires—demands—authenticity from the leader or the more mature Christians in the group. Gone are the days when Christian leaders can clinically sit back behind a large oak desk and help all the less holy Christians with their problems. Depression, moral failures, pride, and a whole host of others sins are committed (or hidden) by Christian leaders and nonleaders alike. We're all screwed up and in desperate need of God's grace. Discipleship groups need to encourage honesty from all participants—especially the leaders.

Second, *take it to the streets.* True discipleship does not take place in a coffee shop or in the pastor's office. There's nothing wrong with dialoguing over a stiff cappuccino, but holistic discipleship must take place *in real life.* Just look at Jesus: He discipled his followers in the ebb and flow of the real world. He helped people become more like him as he was at their home, on the boat, and in the streets where life naturally happened.

In-depth discipleship can't be limited to studying the Bible or praying together. These activities are helpful and needed, but they don't constitute discipleship by themselves. Again, just look at Jesus. How many hours did he spend studying the Bible with his disciples? How often did he pray with them? If you add it all up, it wasn't much. He certainly prayed with them and taught them the Scriptures, but the bulk of his time was spent relating to them in the normal rhythm of life.

One of the best ways to "take discipleship to the streets" is by engaging in a ministry as part of relational discipleship. A youth pastor friend of mine takes his youth group to an urban laundromat once a month on Sundays. They do laundry for all the homeless people in town. For two hours, while the clothes are being washed and dried, the youth engage in conversations with the homeless, share Jesus with them, *relate with them,* and pray for anyone who wants prayer. They also share a meal with them—usually hot biscuits and gravy—while the youth pastor gives a short talk about the gospel.

There are so many things I love about this idea. For one, it's incredibly healthy for teenagers, many of whom have a lot of things handed to them and often feel entitled, to hang out with men with long scruffy beards who reek of urine. It's just good for the soul, and it's not a bad way to fight against consumerism and comfort. But more than this, the youth learn what it means to follow Jesus as they watch their youth pastor follow Jesus. They aren't just hearing about Jesus; they're seeing Jesus both in their discipler and in the people they are serving (Matthew 25:31-46).

The by-product has been beautiful. The youth have built relationships with the homeless, some of whom have come to Christ. The homeless look forward to seeing the youth again because they're treated like friends rather than just ministries. And the youth get a chance to take their faith to the streets and see what Christianity looks like outside the church walls. (More on this in chapter 7.)

Third, *create constructive dialogue.* Relational discipleship must consist of both talking and listening from everyone involved. Healthy relationships always include honest dialogue. People must be free to ask really hard questions and express their deepest doubts and fears.

To be honest, I don't think Gen-Xers (my generation) or Boomers are very good at this. One of my seminary professors—a Boomer—used to say (no joke) that he hated the word *dialogue.* Bible-believing Christians should already know the truth, so there's nothing to "dialogue" about. We should just proclaim the truth and close in prayer. While I appreciate his conviction and courage, it sounds rather arrogant to assume that we have the corner market on "the truth." Certainly, the Bible is true, but accessing that truth requires the messy and fallible process of interpretation. We should therefore hold onto our convictions with humility, being willing to be corrected when we've got it wrong.

Plus, the "I have the truth and I will preach it at you" approach simply doesn't work with Millennials. It feels prideful and naive. Millennials are much more sensitive to the complexity of difficult questions. We're much more effective at helping others become more like Christ when we listen to their perspective and pain, when we engage in the give-and-take of dialogue—asking questions, giving answers, asking more questions.

Fourth, *don't be too focused on discipleship.* Sounds weird, I know. But let me explain it with a story.

My friend Shawn Gordon is an ex-con turned pastor. His life of violence, his gang activity, and a rather successful drug-dealing career landed him twelve years in the most dangerous prisons in America. That's where he met Jesus—or rather, where Jesus met him.

After being released, Shawn was on the streets of San Francisco trying to figure out what it meant to be a Christian in the real world. He had no role model, no mentor, no examples to follow. Twenty-eight days after being released, Shawn met a pastor who invited him to live in his own home. "As a Jesus follower, you're just as close as my own flesh-and-blood family," the pastor said. "Come live with me, and we will follow Jesus together." The pastor had a modest-sized house, a wife, and (at the time) six children. Shawn also had a wife and child. The pastor not only took Shawn and his family in but also told them to stay in his master bedroom for as long as they needed. This is some serious discipleship!

Living with a pastor? They must have read the Bible all day long, I thought. I was shocked when Shawn told me, "We didn't do Bible studies together. We didn't meet for coffee once a week. We didn't do anything all that formal or pro-grammatic. We just lived life together. It is here where I saw what it meant to be a Christian in the daily routine of life."

The pastor happened to be a bestselling author and

famous speaker, Francis Chan. He's a rather busy guy. But instead of using busyness as an excuse not to disciple, Francis invited Shawn into his life as they sought to become more like Christ together. He and his wife, Lisa, just felt that the Spirit of God was telling them to invest in this guy, even though our safety-driven culture was screaming, "Stay as far away as you can!" (I absolutely love the fact that Francis's fame didn't prevent him from giving up his bedroom to some ex-con he just met on the streets—fame seekers take note.)

Shawn now heads up Project Bayview, a holistic discipleship ministry in one of the roughest neighborhoods in San Francisco. Not everyone will be able to invite their disciples to live in their home and sleep in their bed (although, maybe more of us should). But we should all seek to engage in discipleship in the context of real life.

Discipleship is best fostered through organic (natural) conversations that love others as whole people in the rhythm of life where we live out our faith. After all, that's what Jesus did. And when we became Christians, we signed up to become like Jesus, to do the stuff that Jesus did.

4

GOD IN US (NOT JUST IN YOU): THE FULLNESS OF GOD IN COMMUNITY

THE LAST CHAPTER ARGUED—against my fleshly desires—that relationships are vital for one's growth in Christ. This chapter will continue this general theme but will look at it through a slightly different lens: the lens of community.

The Presence of God on Earth

When Jesus called his disciples, he called them into a communal relationship. Jesus didn't select twelve men and disciple them on their own—one on one, with no connection to each other. Rather, he enlisted them as a community of world changers. Jesus didn't come just to save individual sinners. He didn't come just so that you could invite him into your heart. He came to form a community of followers who would carry on his mission to the ends of the earth.

This is seen most explicitly in the Gospel of John. After Jesus washed his disciples' feet, he told them, "You also ought to wash one another's feet" (John 13:14). He then summed up his teaching in terms of loving one another:

> So now I am giving you a new commandment: Love each other. Just as I have loved you, you should love each other. Your love for one another will prove to the world that you are my disciples.
>
> JOHN 13:34-35, NLT

And again:

> This is my commandment: Love each other in the same way I have loved you. There is no greater love than to lay down one's life for one's friends. . . . This is my command: Love each other.
>
> JOHN 15:12-13, 17, NLT

In his high priestly prayer, Jesus asked the Father to ensure that Christians would love each other in unity, that "they may all be one, just as you, Father, are in me, and I in you, that they also may be in us, so that the world may believe that you have sent me" (John 17:21). The truth of Jesus coming to earth will be validated by their unity. "I in them and you in me, that they may become perfectly one, so that the world may know that you sent me and loved them even as you loved me" (John 17:23).

In other words, Christians cannot fully represent Jesus in the world unless they are living in unity with other believers. Our testimony that Jesus is the Savior will be broadcast and validated by how we act *as a community,* not just as individuals.

The New Testament unashamedly and unmistakably celebrates the communal nature of Christianity. There are fifty-nine "one another" commands in the New Testament—eight in the Gospels, thirty-two in Paul's writings, and nineteen in the rest of the New Testament. That's a lot of commands that can't be obeyed in isolation. To live out the Christian faith—to be faithful disciples and be transformed into Christlikeness—we *need* other people. People to love, people to serve, people to relate to, argue with, forgive, enjoy, rebuke, and share our bread and wine with. We can't do it by ourselves.

To live out the Christian faith—to be a faithful disciple and be transformed into Christlikeness—we need other people.

If someone moved to a desert island and lived a perfect moral life, he or she would still be unable to obey many of Jesus's commandments. In some ways, though morally upright, he or she would be a terrible Christian.

Can't Find God on a Mountaintop

It was only a few years ago when I recognized just how biblical the communal nature of Christianity is. For most of my Christian life, I was always taught that to fully experience God, I need to get alone. Steal away a quiet hour by myself. Perhaps I should climb a mountain hours away from other people to experience God.

All of this makes perfect sense to a loner like myself. But then I read the Bible, and I found out that my individualistic desires are contrary to Christianity.

Look at what Paul says in Ephesians: God "put all things under [Jesus'] feet and gave him as head over all things to the church, which is his body, *the fullness of him who fills all in all*" (Ephesians 1:22-23, emphasis added). Think about that. The church—the body of Christ—is "the fullness of God" on earth. Do you want to encounter the fullness of God? Then don't run from God's people to some mountaintop by yourself. The fullness of God resides in the corporate body of Christians. You experience God more fully by engaging Christians, not running from them.

The Christian faith is a communal faith. When God saves you, he saves you *into community.* Jonathan Dodson says it well: "When we are converted, we are not converted to Christ alone . . . we are converted to Christ, to church, and to mission."[1] Disciples of Christ need other disciples of Christ in order to grow closer to Christ and know him in all of his fullness. Paul says this clearly in Ephesians 4, a passage worth quoting at length. Don't just skip it or skim it; read it slowly and follow Paul's logic:

> And he gave the apostles, the prophets, the evangelists, the shepherds and teachers, to equip the saints for the work of ministry, for building up the body of Christ, *until we all attain to the unity of the faith and of the knowledge of the Son of God, to mature manhood, to the measure of the stature of the fullness of Christ,* so that we may no longer be children, tossed

to and fro by the waves and carried about by every
wind of doctrine, by human cunning, by craftiness
in deceitful schemes. Rather, speaking the truth in
love, *we are to grow up in every way into him who
is the head, into Christ, from whom the whole body,
joined and held together by every joint with which
it is equipped, when each part is working properly,
makes the body grow so that it builds itself up in love.*
EPHESIANS 4:11-16, EMPHASIS ADDED

The two parts that I've emphasized capture the point.
If we are to "attain to the unity of the faith" and become
"mature" and grow into the "fullness of Christ," we need to
be in relationships with other believers. If we seek to "grow
up in every way into him"—the stated goal of discipleship—
then we need to engage the body of Christ. It's only when
"each part"—each individual Christian—"is working properly" that the communal body will "build itself up on love."

The Christian faith is communal. You can't go it alone.
Spiritual growth doesn't happen in isolation. Christians
don't—according to the Bible—experience the fullness of
God by themselves. Disciples can only be discipled into
Christlikeness insofar as they are engaging in authentic
relationships with a community of God's people.

This is why I was greatly troubled by what I found in *The
State of Discipleship.*

Rugged Individualism in the Church

According to the Barna study, "Among the nine out of
ten Christians who say spiritual growth is important

(90 percent), more than one-third say they prefer to pursue spiritual growth on their own (37 percent). Similarly, two in five of all Christian adults consider their spiritual life 'entirely private' (41 percent)."[2] Despite their general desire for relationships, Millennials are even more individualistic when it comes to discipleship. "Forty percent of Millennials who consider spiritual growth very or somewhat important prefer on-their-own discipleship, compared with 36 percent among Gen-Xers and 32 percent of Elders (and 39 percent of Boomers, who are more like Millennials in this respect)."[3]

What Is Working?

HOW DO CHRISTIANS WANT TO BE DISCIPLED?

(AMONG THE 9 IN 10 CHRISTIANS WHO SAY SPIRITUAL GROWTH IS IMPORTANT)

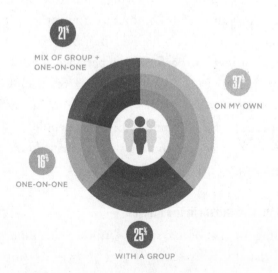

21% MIX OF GROUP + ONE-ON-ONE

37% ON MY OWN

16% ONE-ON-ONE

25% WITH A GROUP

All in all, Christians who desire to grow spiritually have somehow missed the basic biblical theme that spiritual growth happens in community.

Discipleship leaders agree with these statistics. Christians are way too individualistic. Jonathan Dodson writes,

> Churches today have more in common with
> shopping malls. They have become consumerist,
> doctrinaire, lifeless institutions, not Jesus-centered
> missional communities. . . . We have devolved
> from being Jesus-centered communities into loose
> collections of spiritually minded individuals.[4]

Discipleship guru Bill Hull identifies the same problem. "People who claim to be followers of Jesus pack our churches. But they're not connected in community; they try to fly solo."[5] And Greg Ogden observes,

> The church is not immune to the diseases of
> individualism and consumerism dominant in
> American society. . . . To the extent that the church
> is reduced to an aggregate of individuals who shop
> like consumers to meet their needs, we do not have
> the basis for community in any biblical sense.[6]

Why do people who need and desire community not see their faith as essentially communal? There are several probable reasons for this. These aren't the only reasons, but they are at least some of the major ones. We'll look at each problem and offer some possible ways to overcome them in order to create the rich communities necessary to live out our faith.

Technology and Social Media

The State of Discipleship reveals that the omnipresence of technology has hindered our relational engagement—especially among Millennials. For instance, "49 percent of adults 18 to 30 years old acknowledge that their personal electronics separate them from other people." The percentage is lower among other adults, but is still strikingly high: 35 percent of all adults agree that social media and other electronics are hindering their social engagement.[7]

Is technology really making us more isolated and alone? MIT sociologist Sherry Turkle says yes. The opening words of her eye-opening book capture her startling conclusions:

> We are lonely but fearful of intimacy. Digital
> connections and the sociable robot may offer the
> illusion of companionship without the demands
> of friendship. Our networked life allows us to hide
> from each other, even as we are tethered to each
> other. We'd rather text than talk.[8]

Turkle argues that even social media connections through Facebook, Twitter, and Instagram engender superficial relationships, which perpetuates loneliness. Social critic and writer Giles Slade says the same thing about social media in her book *The Big Disconnect: The Story of Technology and Loneliness.*[9] *The State of Discipleship* agrees: "In 2001, about one in eight Americans self-identified as lonely (12 percent).

By 2012, that number had *doubled*—a paradoxical reality in the social-media age."[10]

While technology has the potential to foster relationships, it can't replace real, embodied, face-to-face interaction. Still, we're slavishly relying on technology to satisfy our human longing for intimacy. And it's not working. We're lonelier than ever, and we're becoming more socially stupid. My friend who owns a large company in southern California told me that he rarely hires Millennials for positions in customer service. "It's rare that I interview a twentysomething who knows how to engage with real people."

Suffice it to say that the omnipresence of technology and our addictions to it are stifling communal discipleship. So, how can we overcome technological addiction? We begin by simply addressing it. Exposing it. Modeling that we can live better when we're not enslaved to our gadgets. I think most people deep down know it's a problem, but as long as no one really addresses it, they stay shackled to their devices.

What if churches considered an addiction to technology the same as addiction to alcohol or porn? (There's some overlap there.) What if we preached about it and talked about it in our small groups and other gatherings? What if we created environments where stopping a face-to-face conversation to look at a text would be just as weird as smoking a joint in church?

When Paul says, "Even though 'I am allowed to do anything,' I must not become a slave to anything" (1 Corinthians 6:12, NLT), he was talking specifically about sexual immorality. However, not being "a slave to anything" includes *anything*.

Today, people are enslaved to technology, and it's been proven to hinder us from flourishing in our relationships.

Commuter Culture

The industrial age and the technological revolution have propelled our individualistic spirit. As a result, since World War II America has become a commuter culture. For the first time in history, people rarely live, shop, work, play, and go to church in the same neighborhood. Sociologist Robert Putnam discussed this at length in his groundbreaking book *Bowling Alone*.[11] Our lives don't naturally intersect with people in our communities, since our communities are all over the place. It's not uncommon for people to live in one city, work in another, shop in another, and go to church in yet another. (And Putnam wrote his book in 2001—long before social media became the primary mode of human interaction.)

Before the twentieth century, most people did life within walking distance of everyone else around them. Christians wouldn't just see their brothers and sisters for an hour on Sundays. They crossed paths in their neighborhoods, at the market, in town meetings, and in the fields. Church life was only one small yet vital part of a larger fabric of communal engagement. Christians didn't have to be reminded to "do community"; community was simply a way of life.

There's no way we can turn the tide of culture. We live in a highly mobile age. That's just the way it is. But Christians who desire to become more like Jesus—which can only happen in communal relations with others—need to think deeply about how they can overcome some of these relational barriers.

One thing we could do is encourage people to become part of a church that's close to them. This may not always be possible or even healthy. But I do fear that in our frantic race to fill the sanctuary with as many people as we can, we often don't stop to think, *Maybe there's a closer community that some of these people should get plugged into.* Kingdom-minded Christians don't desire to build *their* kingdom—the local church population. They seek to do what's best for *the* kingdom. And sometimes what's best for the kingdom is for Christians to become part of a community that's close by.

Kingdom-minded Christians don't desire to build their kingdom—the local church population. They seek to do what's best for the kingdom.

Another thing some churches are doing is developing geography-based community groups (or Bible studies, life groups, or whatever we call them). When I was a leader at Cornerstone Church in Simi Valley, they canceled all of their programs and replaced them with community groups that were geographically based. Every square mile of the city had its own midweek community gathering, and the gathering consisted of people who lived within walking distance of each other.

The idea sounded great. And for some groups it was. For others, though, it wasn't too great. The leaders of the church later realized that they changed things around way too quickly—almost overnight! People weren't ready or prepared for the shift. Also, the leaders of the groups weren't adequately prepared. Some groups had gifted leaders, and they generally did pretty well. But other groups didn't have qualified leaders. After all, geography doesn't guarantee that every square mile has a qualified leader who can shepherd the group.

As I reflect back on Cornerstone's radical shift, I actually appreciate it much more now than I did then. I think the pros far outweigh the cons, and, looking back, some of the problems could have been overcome. For one, the geographical boundaries don't need to be so strict. If one neighborhood has three gifted leaders and the next neighborhood has none, then certainly it would be more beneficial for at least one of those leaders to cross the tracks. Likewise, certain people may thrive in a different group. I remember some friends of ours were contemplating leaving their neighborhood group to join ours. We plotted and planned how we could pull this off. We kept it quiet, kept it stealthy. You would have thought we were refugees seeking to hop the border!

The point is not to be legalistic about geography. Churches can promote and encourage proximity-based gatherings while allowing some fluidity amongst the groups. Too much fluidity could lead to consumerism, where people pick and choose groups based on whom they like rather than whom God wants them to be with. But strict proximity with no fluidity could feel legalistic and stifling, especially when the Spirit may want to connect people who don't live by each other.

These details will need to be worked through, but we should all recognize that mobility *can* hinder community.

There's no pat answer to the problem. But we'd be naïve not to recognize that there is a problem.

Noncommunal Communities

Part of the reason why many Christians would rather keep their spiritual lives to themselves is that they haven't experienced rich, vibrant community. Maybe they are welcomed by a smiley greeter at the door, or perhaps they had a passing conversation on their way to pick up their kids from Sunday school. Maybe they tried to connect with other believers at a Bible study, but those connections never made it below the surface. The fact is, many (perhaps most) believers never experience the depth of community envisioned in the New Testament.

Imagine a community where you are treated as family. When you weep, they weep. When you laugh, they laugh. When you lose your job, everyone pitches in to cover your rent. Imagine being known as you really are and still loved in spite of who you really are. No addictions, no struggles, no deep dirty secrets can pry your family away from you. Forgiveness and grace hang in the air so thickly that you can chew it. And you all rally around a world-changing cause so invigorating that it binds you together more passionately than a packed house at a Green Bay Packers game.

If you had access to that kind of community, would you really want to do it alone? No one really wants to go bowling alone. We only do it because we've never experienced a better option.

I know what you're thinking, and you're partially right. The type of community I described is idealistic. Maybe it reflects what the church is *supposed* to be, but it's unreal. It doesn't exist. This is true. This side of heaven, no church community will perfectly exist the way God intended it. The problem, though, is not that many churches are just falling short of the ideal. It's that they often look nothing like it.

No Community without a King

Unfortunately, the greatest deterrent to biblical community is invisible. Our current conception of the "gospel" is anemic! We must acknowledge our confinement of the "gospel" to personal justification, and then realign our understanding of the gospel to match the biblical narrative.

Although the gospel includes an offer of justification and reconciliation, in its largest sense it is a proclamation that the kingdom of God has come. True biblical community only flourishes where we see ourselves as fellow subjects of God's kingdom, submitted in fealty to the same King and his mission. In other words, community is not the *impetus* for mission; it arises in the *context* of mission.

FRAN SCIACCA, author of *So, What's Your Point?*

Sociologists Josh Packard and Ashleigh Hope reveal some startling truths in their book *Church Refugees*. After extensive interviews with dozens of "dechurched" Christians—who left the church but not the faith—Packard and Hope discovered a common theme. These people longed for intimate relationships, but they didn't experience such relationships in church. According to one interviewee, church "was very corporate just in how it managed people and how it set up programs. To me it was just like a big transaction, and the big thing especially to me, is that it was very impersonal."[12] Lack of intimate relationships is a common theme throughout their book. The "dechurched value relationships and community above everything" and "see their human relationships as an extension of their relationships with the divine."[13]

On a more anecdotal level, most Christians I talk to feel disconnected at church. Some feel completely isolated and alone. Just yesterday I talked to a pastor of a large and vibrant church who said that almost everyone he's talked to at church feels disconnected from other believers in church. They're not truly known. I've been startled by the increasing number of people I meet who feel this way. You wouldn't guess it if you saw them on Sunday mornings. Smiles are exchanged. Conversations are tossed around. You may even overhear someone mutter the token "I'll pray for you." But if they were depressed, lonely, struggling with an addiction, or contemplating suicide, or if they had just had a major fight with their spouse, no one would know it.

Churches will always fall short of the ideal. But it's possible, even this side of heaven, to create a community that no one wants to leave.

Individualistic Language and Theology

External pressures like technology and mobility aren't the only things that hinder community. Some of the problems are internal, such as how we talk about church and how we describe our relationship with God. Our Christian language reveals and perpetuates the individualistic theology we say we're trying to overcome. Just think about some of our common phrases:

- *"Accept Jesus into your heart."* This is an individualistic idea. Jesus is the King of kings and sits at the right hand of the Father in heaven. We don't accept him into our heart; we acknowledge his lordship over all things. Using this phrase reinforces our individualism.
- *"Having a personal relationship with Jesus."* This phrase has some truth to it as long as we don't understand "personal" to mean "private." Our relationship with Jesus is personal, but it's never *just* personal. It's also communal and missional.
- *"Going to church."* This phrase might not strike you as individualistic, but the way we often use it sounds like a bunch of individuals attending an event. This galvanizes the idea that church is more like a baseball game or a concert than a family gathering. "How was the Dodgers game?" "Good!" "How was church?" "Good!"

Even the widespread notion of having "private devotions," where believers read the Bible and pray by themselves, nurtures an individualistic approach to spiritual growth. It's striking that before the printing press (circa AD 1450), most Christians were illiterate, and even the literate ones rarely owned their own personal Bible. Most people couldn't afford one. This means that Christianity has grown and flourished for hundreds of years *without most of its followers ever reading the Bible on their own.* How did they know God's Word? Through community. Literate Christians would spend hours reading and studying the Bible in community with other believers. Communal gatherings weren't icing on the cake. They were essential to one's faith. You couldn't get very far in the faith without depending on fellow brothers and sisters in Christ.

The same goes for prayer. While in some cases we see Jesus and other people in the Bible praying individually, most of the prayers of the Bible are corporate. Even certain psalms that contain individual prayers were compiled into a Psalter (the "book of Psalms") and used as corporate prayer and worship. Though the Bible contains individual expressions of the faith, these are the exceptions, not the norm.

I'm not saying we should do away with individual Bible reading and prayer. God forbid! These are a healthy part of our discipleship. But they are only a part. One cannot grow as a disciple by individual Bible reading and prayer alone. Remember how Paul defined *growth* in Ephesians 4: Spiritual growth is intrinsically *communal.* We must study the Bible in community, pray "we" prayers more often than "I" prayers, and view ourselves as small parts of a larger body—the body of Christ. Using biblical language, which is often corporate, instead of modern individualistic Christian clichés will help reinforce our communal identity.

The One-Third Gospel

Jonathan Dodson helpfully describes the individualism in the church as a "one-third gospel."

> This one-third gospel is hardly the gospel at all. It focuses on Jesus's death and resurrection as a doctrine to be believed, not on Jesus as a Person to be trusted and obeyed. The gospel has been reduced to a personal ticket to heaven. But the biblical gospel is much more than personal conversion to gain a reservation in heaven. It is conversion to Jesus Christ as Lord. Moreover, the gospel has two more "thirds." The gospel calls us into *community* and on to *mission*.[14]

One way we can turn the tide of individualism is by making much of the other two-thirds of the gospel. Talk about it, preach about it, teach it to your children. When we only preach a one-third gospel and people get saved, it becomes way more difficult to try to slip in the other two-thirds down the road. Jesus told his seekers to "count the cost" before they made a decision to follow him. The other two-thirds are part of that cost that people need to count. We need to be clear that part of making a decision to follow Christ is making a commitment to join the *community* of God's people and venture into the *mission* that God calls us to.

In other words, we need to preach, live, teach, embrace, and celebrate a more holistic gospel. So let's unpack what that holistic gospel looks like.

ON EARTH AS IT IS IN HEAVEN

I WANT YOU TO MEET my friend Barry.[1] Barry is a Christian who owns a factory. He desires to have the gospel shape everything he does. Instead of maximizing profits at all costs, Barry believes that people come before profits. Even though he could maximize the company's profits by paying his employees twelve dollars an hour, he pays them fifteen dollars instead. He doesn't pay them more so that he can get them to produce more. Rather, he pays them more because, as image bearers of God, they are worth it.

Barry values people and family more than work. This is why he requires people to work seven hours a day instead of eight, and he gives every employee the third Friday off every month so they can spend time with their families or in the community.

Since Barry's God doesn't view people through a hierarchical lens, neither does he. So instead of structuring the factory's pay scale based on hierarchy, he structures it based on need. Barry is the CEO, but he only has two kids. The janitor has six kids, one of whom is special needs and another who has an expensive medical condition. Instead of paying the janitor a typical janitor's wage, Barry pays him more than he pays himself—since the janitor's needs are much greater than Barry's.

Barry also knows that immigrants and refugees have a hard time finding jobs, especially if they don't know English very well. The patriotic side of Barry believes that "it's every man for himself" and "if you're going to come to my country, then you'd better learn the language." But Barry's Christian side wins out. Jesus commanded his followers to make disciples of all nations, and God is bringing the nations here. So Barry goes out of his way to provide jobs and English training for immigrants and refugees, believing that a multicultural community—even at a factory—best reflects the heart of God. Barry also recognizes that caring for the stranger and alien is a clear biblical theme, so he integrates this biblical theme into this vocation.

Question: how many hours a week does Barry put into his spiritual growth?

Some people would need more information. "How many hours does Barry spend in church on Sunday and Bible study on Tuesday? Is he in a Christian book club? Is he doing his devotions? Is he listening to Christian worship music on his way to work?" I would argue that much of Barry's week is filled with spiritual growth because he's integrating the gospel into every fiber of his vocation.

When your entire vocation is viewed as mission, there are very few hours that *aren't* discipleship. There's certainly a place for typical discipleship activities. But we've got to move beyond thinking of discipleship in terms of how many hours we spend doing church activities and engaging in spiritual alone time. Discipleship is a way of life—all of life.

Until we can explore how the gospel affects all areas of life, we won't be cultivating holistic disciples.

Shattering the Sacred/Secular Divide

Many Christians function with a secular/sacred divide.[2] They consider discipleship to be an important part of the *sacred* aspects of life (attending church, going to Bible study, praying in the morning), but they don't know how it relates to their so-called *secular* lives—their careers, hobbies, or forms of entertainment. Few Christians, it seems, view discipleship as a holistic endeavor, where we become like Christ in the way we think about art, beauty, economics, immigration, and science (among other things).

According to *The State of Discipleship,* most Christians view their "spiritual lives" as a private matter. The study reveals that 41 percent of Christians consider their spiritual lives to be "entirely private." Only 37 percent consider their spiritual lives to have "an impact on relatives"; 36 percent say it has "an impact on friends"; 33 percent say it has "an impact on [their] community"; and 29 percent say it should have "an impact on society."[3] While the previous chapter shows that many Christians would rather pursue Jesus by themselves,

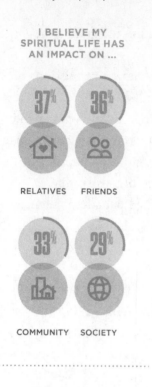

I BELIEVE MY
SPIRITUAL LIFE HAS
AN IMPACT ON ...

37%   36%

RELATIVES   FRIENDS

33%   29%

COMMUNITY   SOCIETY

I BELIEVE MY
SPIRITUAL LIFE IS
ENTIRELY PRIVATE

41%

these stats show that many Christians think that their faith should impact only themselves.

Despite such compartmentalization, there's a growing hunger to connect the gospel to all of life. While some Millennials still try to pursue Christ on their own, many of them desire to explore a more holistic gospel. Most people are passionate about their vocation, and the same is true for Millennials. The Barna study shows that 37 percent of Millennials expect to make an impact through their work within the first five years, and another 28 percent expect to do so in six or more years. Churches can nurture this passion and help Millennials stay connected to Christ by focusing on vocational *calling* outside of traditional church-based ministry. According to Barna: "Millennials who have remained active in their faith (45 percent) are three times more likely than church dropouts (17 percent) to say they learned to view their gifts and passions as part of God's calling."[4]

In other words, to help people stay connected to Jesus,

churches should teach people how the gospel connects to all of life—especially their vocation.

David Kinnaman shows that most Christians still think that the gospel affects only their moral or spiritual lives; the bulk of their Monday-through-Saturday lives remain untouched by the Good News. Many Christians feel

> that their vocation (or professional calling) is disconnected from their church experience. Their Christian background has not prepared them to live and work effectively in society. Their faith is "lost" from Monday through Friday. The Christianity they have learned does not meaningfully speak to the fields of fashion, finance, medicine, science, or media to which they are drawn.[5]

That second-to-last one is important: science. According to Kinnaman's study, 52 percent of Christian teens in youth groups aspire to science-related careers, and yet only 1 percent of youth pastors addressed issues related to faith and science over the course of an entire year.[6] Part of the problem is that many churches tend to demonize the sciences for fear that Christians will lose their faith and become evolutionists. But the church should not be fearful of science; rather, it should learn how to thoughtfully engage the scientific world around it—a world that many of its members will be living in.

While we're on the subject of faith and science, we might as well name the elephant in the room: The whole question of faith and science has become incredibly volatile and fear driven. This has caused many churches to either ignore the hard questions that people have or fail to create space for constructive dialogue and healthy disagreement. In my own experience as a Christian and theologian, I've seen many believers turn nonessential questions about the age of the earth or the interpretation of Genesis 1–2 into gospel truths. "If you disagree with a particular view, then you're a heretic and can't be a real Christian," some say.

One's interpretation of Genesis 1–2 does not have to be a gospel issue. In fact, I've met several people who resisted Christianity largely because they thought they had to hold to a particular view of the age of the earth. When they found out that genuine Christians disagree on this question and that they didn't need to believe that the earth was only six thousand years old in order to worship Jesus, they got saved.

The point is, churches need to resist being controlled by fear-driven rhetoric and to explore ways in which they can nurture and train people to think critically about matters of faith and science. If the church doesn't do it, the university will.

More and more people deeply desire to connect the gospel to all of life. They "want to follow Jesus in a way that connects with the world they inhabit, to partner with God outside the walls of the church, and to pursue Christianity without separating themselves form the world."[7] In other words, they don't want to maintain the secular/sacred divide, since all of life is sacred. Kinnaman points out that many of these people "are also creative types—artists, musicians, entertainers, and filmmakers—who feel their calling is out of tune with their Christian upbringing. *They think the church doesn't know what to do with creatives like them.*"[8]

My friend Sean Michel is one of these creative types. Sean is a killer musician who hasn't cut his hair or his beard in ten years. (Imagine: ZZ Top meets Phil Robertson without the duck call.) The dude absolutely shreds on the guitar and has a voice that makes Bono sound off-key. And Sean loves Jesus. He lives his life to glorify the name of Christ. But here's the thing: Sean doesn't play your typical kind of church music. There's not much of a market in the Christian music industry for homeless-looking musicians playing ramped-up Southern Rock ten decibels too loud. So Sean plays at bars, clubs, and other venues that are filled with unbelievers. His lyrics are laced with aggressive theological themes that exalt Jesus' name to the high heavens. Just look up "Sean Michel Hosea Blues" on YouTube, and you'll find a gritty modern-day rendition of God's grace written about in the book of Hosea, set to a heart-thumping beat that sounds like stuff you'd hear in a club.

Sean doesn't believe in the secular/sacred divide. He believes that excellent music played in secular places can usher in the sacred presence of Christ.

Despite this growing desire to connect the gospel to all of life (especially vocation), church leaders still seem to be too narrowly focused on discipleship as church activities. When pastors were asked how many members are involved in discipleship, they said about 40 percent. Discipleship leaders were slightly more optimistic: 50 percent of church members, they say, are involved in a discipleship activity. But the way discipleship was measured was in terms of certain church activities such as attending Sunday school or fellowship group, meeting with a spiritual mentor, studying the

Bible with a group, or reading and discussing a Christian book with a group.[9] When leaders were asked to estimate how much time their members spent "doing something to further their spiritual growth," they said "about three hours per week."[10] I fear that they might confront Sean for not taking his faith very seriously, since he's out at some bar on Saturday night instead of attending Christian book club.

A Holistic Christian View of Vocation

When God created humanity, the first two commands he gave them were to "be fruitful and multiply" and to "have dominion over" the earth (Genesis 1:28). Or in urban lingo, "Have lots of sex and rule the world." Not a bad gig, if you ask me. Anyway, that second command, to reign over the earth, is fundamental to our humanity. It has tremendous implications for our understating of vocation. When God put Adam and Eve in the Garden of Eden, he told them "to tend and watch over it" (Genesis 2:15, NLT)—in other words, to cultivate it, develop it, harness it, and expand it.[11] Adam and Eve's work in the garden was a way of "reigning over" the earth.

The same is true for us. God put us on the earth so that we would *mediate God's rule over the world.* God didn't scrap his original plan when Adam sinned. He still wants us to apply God's way of doing things to all areas of life, including our vocation.

I love how the end of the Bible picks up from the beginning. In Revelation 21–22, we see a new creation that looks a whole lot like Eden. There are rivers, vegetation, and human flourishing; there's even a tree of life (Revelation 22:1-2). God's plan to rule the world through humanity will be accomplished in the end. The meek will "inherit the earth," Jesus says (Matthew 5:5). Or in the words of the heavenly choir: "You have made them a kingdom and priests to our God, and *they shall reign on the earth*" (Revelation 5:10, emphasis added). There will be quite a few hiccups between Genesis and Revelation, but the mandate remains the same. We all have vocations and callings in our lives, and God calls us to rule them well. The famed Dutch theologian Abraham Kuyper cried out, "There is not a square inch in the whole domain of our human existence over which Christ, who is Sovereign over all, does not cry, Mine!"[12]

Jesus didn't come preaching a gospel of individual salvation, nor did he come to take us to church. He came preaching "the kingdom of God"—the reign of God over all things. When Jesus announced the gospel of the kingdom (Matthew 4:23), he wasn't just talking about the forgiveness of sins and going to heaven when we die. These things are included, of course. But his message of the kingdom can't be limited to these things. Jesus' kingdom message announced a new way of life, where the sick are healed, poor are fed, outcasts are included, and enemies and neighbors are loved. Jesus' kingdom is a whole new reality, a different way of living, a countercultural existence that can't be contained inside the four walls of a church building.

Jesus' kingdom is a whole new reality, a different way of living, a countercultural existence that can't be contained inside the four walls of a church building.

If you're a Christian, you're part of God's kingdom. And you don't leave this kingdom behind when you go to work. Remember Kuyper's declaration: Every square inch—including your Monday-to-Friday routine—belongs to Jesus.

Integrating the Gospel into All of Life

So how do we do this? How can churches cultivate a broader, more holistic, view of discipleship?

Believe and teach a holistic gospel. It starts by actually believing that the sacred/secular divide is not what God intended. When pastors and leaders become passionate about connecting the gospel to all areas of life, this mindset will trickle down. If you want a great example of how to go about this, check out the lengthy sermon series connecting the gospel to vocation from John Mark Comer, teaching pastor of Bridgetown: A Jesus Church in Portland.[13]

Some will resist this message. There are Christians who are always scared when they hear something about Christianity that they hadn't considered before. They equate "new" or "different" with liberal, sinful, and ungodly. I remember hearing a retired Bible professor tell a younger professor, "I'm getting nervous with all of this kingdom talk." The younger professor had been teaching about Jesus' holistic gospel, and he kept emphasizing the concept of kingdom more than (not instead of) the salvation of individuals. The younger professor was humble enough not to smugly remind the older professor that such "kingdom talk" is rooted in Jesus, who talked an awful lot about the kingdom. The older professor was so committed to winning individuals to Christ that he didn't have the mental space to broaden (not change) his perspective, even if this "new" perspective came from Christ's own preaching.

Some people will get nervous when you apply the gospel

(and therefore discipleship) to all of life. But most Christians, especially Millennials, will appreciate it. As we saw from Kinnaman's study, Millennials desire to understand the significance of their vocation. "Despite years of church-based experiences and countless hours of Bible-centered teaching, millions of next-generation Christians have no idea that their faith connects to their life's work."[14] In the absence of good, holistic discipling, the significance of their vocation has remained a mystery, an untested assumption. A holistic gospel gives them eyes to see the kingdom at work in the work they do.

Empower the outliers. Every church has outliers—people who don't quite fit the mold. I'm not talking about unbelievers who try out church for a while but then leave because they don't actually love Jesus. I'm talking about zealous Christians, passionate believers, people who would much rather feed the poor than listen to yet another sermon.

My cousin Paul is one of these outliers. From the time he was nineteen years old, he was a rebel, but he was also a Christian. He tried to attend a conservative Christian college, but they kept telling him to cut his hair so it wouldn't touch his collar. (After three haircuts, he finally got it right.) He dropped out after a year, not because he didn't love Jesus but because he didn't fit into this Christian subculture. "I just couldn't play that game. I wanted to spend my energy engaging in meaningful work." He thought about becoming a pastor, but the thought of preparing and preaching sermons to Christians every Sunday seemed like a nightmare. He wasn't really into "church" as it's traditionally understood.

Paul ended up finding one of the most unreached countries in the world. I'd tell you the name of the country, but it could get him killed. He bought a plane ticket, and that's where he's spent the bulk of his life—pursuing a mission that 99 percent of Christians would never think of doing. He was run out of the country by terrorists a couple of years ago, but he's now returned with his wife and two small children. He's spreading the gospel in a gospel-less land by creating small businesses that provide jobs in an impoverished country. Jesus' kingdom is breaking into this unreached country through the radical missional ventures of a wild-eyed outlier.

My friend Josh Stump is another outlier. He's a pastor and church planter who has planted several churches in the Nashville area. Nashville is an interesting place. There are more churches in Nashville than delis in New York. It's the Vatican of the Bible Belt. But the churches there are largely focused on reaching middle-class suburb dwellers. Josh's heart is for the outcast, the marginalized, and the ones who would never set foot inside a megachurch, even if it has a great sound system. And Josh is the right guy to do it. Although he's a pastor, he owns a cigar shop in east Nashville (the part of Nashville that you probably didn't visit when you were touring the city). Selling (and smoking) cigars is his full-time job. If you entered his shop, you'd never know that he's a pastor. He's got more tattoos than Elvis had shoes, and his hipster beard puts David Crowder to shame.

"You know, Preston," Josh told me, "I talk about Jesus and do more pastoring here in this cigar shop than I do at my church."

"Your church sounds pretty Christless," I gibed back.

Josh laughed with a lingering grin and kept going. "My customers don't just come to smoke cigars. They come for relationships, community, and to talk about religion. Yet they would never go to a traditional church. And I fear that if they did go to a traditional church, they wouldn't engage in the same depth of spiritual conversations that they do here in my shop."

Boldly Following God into Our Neighborhoods

Leaders of the "new parish" movement recognize that advancing the gospel and helping people grow as followers of Jesus cannot be accomplished with a few ministry events and one-on-one meetings. We see ourselves as servants of our neighborhood, working for hope, healing, and justice, in faith that the local place is the context in which God's kingdom flourishes.

Our vision is that these laborers be "rooted incarnationally in their local context." Most ministry training, however, doesn't equip leaders with the skills to investigate the uniqueness of God's work within particular communities and within their own personal stories. These leaders often feel adrift and alone as their creative imagination for the kingdom of God fades. Nav Neighbors supports leaders as like-minded practitioners, boldly following God into our neighborhoods and listening well to God's desire for shalom there.

AL ENGLER, Nav Neighbors mission director

He's right. As I sat there in his shop, coughing on a cigar, I kept seeing customer (friend) after customer (friend) wanting to engage in meaningful conversation with Josh. Religion, politics, sports, cigars, barbecue—they were all fair game. But it wasn't long before Jesus came up in conversation. Josh's Monday-through-Friday vocation is saturated with the presence of Jesus, whose glory shines through a smoke-filled room filled with misfits.

My friend Tasha was raised in a Christian home that was anything but Christlike. I'll save you the details. Let's just say that she was so spiritually abused that I'm surprised she's still a Christian. Tasha's not your typical churchgoer. She's an outlier. She attends Sunday services, but beyond that she would score pretty low on the discipleship activity meter. She's tried out various Bible studies and women's groups, but they just don't fit her. Maybe she should attend anyway, or maybe she should do something different. She's always wrestling with her place in the church.

One day my wife was hanging out with Tasha in her neighborhood. As they were walking Tasha's daughter to school, at least half a dozen women greeted her. "Hey, Tasha, thanks for bringing that meal last night!" "Tasha, thanks for praying with me yesterday." "Hey Tasha, are we having our knitting group tonight?"

My wife was amazed. She had no idea. She never knew that Tasha had invested so much time and relational energy in the unbelievers in her neighborhood—people who would never set foot in a church. She's been running that knitting group now for a couple years, and all of her friends who attend are unbelievers. "Some of them are starting to ask questions about religion!" Tasha said with childlike joy.

Tasha doesn't fit the typical Christian subculture. She'd

probably have a great time talking about Jesus at Josh's cigar shop.

Every church has its outliers. They're zealous for their faith, but they seek to live it out in unconventional ways. They're often creative, energetic, and eager to reach the lost. They would rather be with unbelievers than with Christians, especially Christians who would judge them for not going to church more often. Many of these outliers end up leaving the church. They're hungry to pursue God's mission, yet they find that the church often stifles their passion.

A church that believes in holistic discipleship will empower its outliers. Rather than seeing them as a threat or a nuisance, holistic churches will value them and the unique call God has placed on them. Discipleship doesn't come with some prepackaged formula that looks the same for all people. Rather, it meets people where they're at and honors the diversity of God's calling.

Some people are called to be pastors. Others are called to run cigar shops. Both are called to ministry. And it's the church's job to "equip the saints for the work of ministry" (Ephesians 4:12).

Asset-based discipleship. One of the biggest complaints among church leaders is that people are not engaged in discipleship. According to *The State of Discipleship,* pastors give various reasons why: "lack of commitment" (87 percent), "too much busyness in their lives" (85 percent), "sinful habits" (70 percent), and "pride that inhibits teachability" (70 percent) are the most common reasons church leaders give.[15] What's interesting is that Christian adults don't give the same reasons for their lack of participation in discipleship activities. For instance, while 85 percent of church leaders say that "busyness" is the main obstacle for discipleship, only 23 percent of Christian adults said the same.[16]

Could it be that church leaders only *think* that people aren't participating because they're too busy? Perhaps there are other reasons that leaders aren't aware of.

TOP BARRIERS TO SPIRITUAL GROWTH

● PRACTICING CHRISTIANS ● NON-PRACTICING CHRISTIANS

4% 6%	5% 6%	5% 7%	5% 8%	11% 8%	8% 10%
I HAVEN'T FOUND ANYONE WILLING TO HELP ME	IT'S HARD TO FIND GOOD RESOURCES OR INFORMATION	I DON'T KNOW WHERE TO START	MY FAMILY MEMBERS ARE NOT SUPPORTIVE	MY FRIENDS ARE NOT AS INTERESTED IN SPIRITUAL THINGS	I HAVE OTHER MORE IMPORTANT PRIORITIES RIGHT NOW

10% 12%	16% 13%	9% 15%	9% 16%	6% 16%	23% 22%
I DON'T WANT TO THINK ABOUT MISTAKES I'VE MADE IN THE PAST	SPIRITUAL GROWTH WILL REQUIRE A LOT OF HARD WORK	I DON'T WANT TO GET TOO PERSONAL WITH OTHER PEOPLE	I'VE HAD BAD PAST EXPERIENCES WITH GROUPS OR INDIVIDUALS	I CAN'T FIND A GOOD CHURCH OR CHRISTIAN COMMUNITY	GENERAL BUSYNESS OF LIFE

Josh Packard and Ashleigh Hope addressed this very question in their book *Church Refugees*. Josh recalls talking to a pastor who complained, "People are just too busy to do anything. . . . They say they want things, but they don't want to have to do any of it." I love Josh's response: "The sociologist in me has always bristled at these arguments."[17] Josh suggests that maybe churches are creating programs, ministries, and discipleship activities from the top down, rather from the ground up. In other words, what the leaders think people need to be engaged in may not actually align with the diversity of callings that God has placed on the hearts of his people.

It's the church's job to harness and equip the gifts and passions of the body of Christ. But to do this, you have to begin by actually asking the body, "What do you *want* to do to make disciples of all nations?" Maybe it's a neighborhood knitting group. Maybe it's a laundry ministry to the homeless. Or maybe it's sharing the love of Christ through art therapy. (One interviewee in Josh's research helps people encounter the healing power of Christ through art.)

Josh talks about utilizing the principles of asset-based community development (ABCD) and applying it to the church's discipleship.[18] Asset-based community development "focuses on identifying and leveraging the strengths that currently exist in a community rather than focusing on its deficits and problems."[19] Instead of creating certain one-size-fits-all discipleship programs, an ABCD approach seeks to empower the unique gifts and passions of the people under your care. What if God has put in your congregation fifteen people who smoke cigars and have a fiery passion for the whiskey-drinking hipsters in your community? Telling them to join a Christian book club and then complaining that they're "too busy" when they don't show up isn't going to help them become more like Christ.

Becoming Like Jesus—Holistically

Remember, Christ was dangerous and unpredictable. He didn't play by the religious rules. He planted a church with hit men and treasonists at his side. He was so close to drunkards and gluttons that the religious elite thought he was one (Matthew 11:19). He wasn't afraid to go to a party filled with scoundrels who didn't have a moral bone in their bodies (Luke 5:29-32). If we are going to "become like Christ" in the way we disciple and are discipled, we may need to set aside our seminary notes and start from scratch—or start from the Bible. And then start with the passions and callings of the people. "The Dones," as Josh Packard calls them, "demonstrated to us time and time again that they're capable, talented, and driven." He's talking about their passion for the kingdom of God, their desire to touch a lost and dying world with the love of Christ. "They want the church to draw on their assets, not provide them with services."[20]

A holistic approach to discipleship will break free from the shackles of "the way we've always done things" and explore new avenues to empower diverse people to live out God's call to rule the world. The typical discipleship activities are important; we shouldn't do away with church services and Bible studies. But we need to augment these forms of traditional Christianity with creative forms of empowerment, where diverse expressions of the Christian faith are not judged but enlisted into service for establishing God's kingdom on earth as it is in heaven.

6

LOVING GOD WITH YOUR MIND

THE GOAL OF DISCIPLESHIP IS TRANSFORMATION. Discipleship is not just about gaining head-knowledge about God or the Bible, and it's not just about getting people to attend more discipleship activities. It's about Jesus—and helping people become more like him.

The State of Discipleship reveals that both church leaders and adult Christians agree with this sentiment. When asked about the goals of discipleship, most senior pastors said it was "being transformed to become more like Jesus" (87 percent), followed by "growing in spiritual maturity" (79 percent) and "knowing Christ more deeply" (78 percent). Adult Christians were a little less explicit, but they chose phrases that generally involved some sort of life transformation. The goal of discipleship is "learning to live a more consistent Christian life" (60 percent), "learning to trust in God more" (59 percent), and "knowing Christ more deeply" (58 percent). The Barna study concludes that "church leaders who embrace a culture of discipleship describe a shift away from 'head knowledge' toward life transformation . . . [and] leaders and Christians alike prefer the term 'becoming more Christ-like'."[1]

Every discipleship leader I've consulted agrees. It's like a broken record. Discipleship is not just about learning or studying or attending a program. It's about life transformation, learning to live like Jesus.

TOP 3 GOALS FOR DISCIPLESHIP

PASTORS AND LAYPEOPLE HAVE VERY DIFFERENT GOALS FOR DISCIPLESHIP

1. LEARNING TO LIVE A MORE CONSISTENT CHRISTIAN LIFE
2. LEARNING TO TRUST IN GOD MORE
3. KNOWING CHRIST MORE DEEPLY

1. BEING TRANSFORMED TO BECOME MORE LIKE JESUS
2. GROWING IN SPIRITUAL MATURITY
3. KNOWING CHRIST MORE DEEPLY

CHRISTIANS ●
PASTORS ●

As the vice president of a Bible college, I often meet up with pastors to tell them about our school. Sometimes I feel like a salesman as I advertise our affordable tuition, relational environment, and commitment to the authority of Scripture.

At this point, pastors are only somewhat impressed. After all, they've heard all of this before.

But it never fails. It happens every time. Pastors perk up and lean into the conversation whenever I talk about transformation: "At Eternity Bible College, we're committed to reaching the heart, not just the mind. We have no desire to just fill our students with head knowledge. We teach in order to transform lives. If our students are not growing in love and humility and service toward one another, then they're not truly learning."

I usually just stop talking at that point because pastors love to continue the thought. After all, this is why they chose to go into the ministry. They want to see lives changed, not just minds filled. They want to see people transformed, not just informed.

But I fear that in an admirable effort to emphasize transformation, we may have swung the pendulum too far in the other direction. We may be neglecting a vital aspect of discipleship—being a learner and thinker. Discipleship is more than just learning and thinking. It's about transformation. But to experience true transformation, we've got to pursue learning and thinking.

Disciple as Learner

The Greek word for disciple, *mathetes,* actually means "learner" in its earliest usage. The word first occurs in the work of fifth century BC Greek historian Herodotus, and after him Plato, Aristotle, Xenophon, and other classical writers use the term *mathetes* to refer to a student of music, astronomy, writing, hunting, wrestling, or other areas of study. The Sophists (an ancient philosophical school) used the term *mathetes* simply to mean "student."[2]

In Jesus' day, the word *mathetes* was used much more broadly to refer to anyone devoted to a significant leader or teacher. Jesus adopted this broader meaning as well. But notice that the aspect of *learning* is never left behind. Jesus didn't do away with "learning." He simply added "imitation" to it. After all, a significant portion of Jesus' ministry—his discipleship—included teaching (Matthew 5–7; 10; 13; 18; 24–25). "Come to me, all who labor and are heavy laden," Jesus said, "and learn from me" (Matthew 11:28-29). In one of the most significant statements he ever made about discipleship, Jesus mandated *teaching* disciples to do what he said:

> Go therefore and make disciples of all nations,
> baptizing them in the name of the Father and
> of the Son and of the Holy Spirit, *teaching them*
> to observe all that I have commanded you.
>
> MATTHEW 28:19-20, EMPHASIS ADDED

You can't be a disciple who makes disciples without some form of teaching.

I love what Paul says to the Ephesian believers. He addresses some sins that they should avoid, sins that unbelievers are engaging in (Ephesians 4:17-19). Then he says, "But that isn't what you *learned* about Christ" (4:20, NLT, emphasis added). Paul's challenge to avoid sin and pursue righteousness—transformation—is rooted in learning about Christ. He goes on to say, "Since you have heard about Jesus and have *learned the truth that comes from him,* throw off your old sinful nature and your former way of life" (4:21-22, emphasis added). For Paul, learning should lead to transformation, and transformation can't be achieved without learning.

As in Ephesians 4, Paul cradles transformation with learning:

> Don't copy the behavior and customs of this world, but let God transform you into a new person *by changing the way you think.* Then you will *learn to know* God's will for you, which is good and pleasing and perfect.
>
> ROMANS 12:2, NLT, EMPHASIS ADDED

It's not an either/or (thinking or transformation) for Paul. Divine transformation happens through "changing the way you think."

The Scandal of the Evangelical Mind

In 1995, evangelical historian Mark Noll published his provocative and highly acclaimed book *The Scandal of the Evangelical Mind.*[3] The book won *Christianity Today's* book-of-the-year award and has been hailed as one of the most important Christian books of its decade. After meticulously examining the evangelical tradition, Noll summed up his findings with his now-famous conclusion: "The scandal of the evangelical mind is that there is not much of an evangelical mind."

Years later, Noll acknowledged that things have improved

a bit—but only a bit.[4] Evangelicals are still plagued by an anti-intellectual spirit, and it shows. As we saw in chapter 1, the American church experiences an embarrassing level of biblical illiteracy despite having instant access to the Bible in several forms. It's difficult to live out Christian values when you don't know what those values are.

But the problem runs much deeper than just biblical illiteracy. Knowing the Bible's content is important, but this doesn't constitute the entirety of Christian learning. In order to "be transformed by the renewing of your mind," we need to learn *how* to think, not just *what* to think.

All of the researchers who have studied both the "Dones" and the Millennial flight from church expose the same important truth: The church has done a poor job at thoughtfully engaging the pressing issues of the day. From science to sexuality, Christians are being told what to think, not how to think. Apologist Walter Martin used to say, "When we fail to give people good answers to their questions, we become another reason for them to disbelieve."[5] The key word there is *good*. It's not that Christians don't give answers. The problem is that the answers are not always good ones, and Millennials in particular can sniff out a thoughtless answer a mile away.

At Eternity Bible College, one of our values is "education not indoctrination." Indoctrination is when Christians are told to memorize the "right" answer, which means whatever the professor thinks is right. Instead, Eternity Bible College seeks to educate its students, training them how to think so that when they go out into the real world and don't have a college professor at their side, they'll be able to think critically and Christianly through all areas of life. It just so happens that a major complaint from the "Dones" is that the church doesn't educate; it only indoctrinates. One "Done" named Emily said, "I've always had questions for the church, but there isn't much room in Christian churches and denominations to question." Another "Done" said that Christians in church "were only interested in my questions so they could answer them, and they thought they had all the answers."[6]

Again, authenticity is a high value for most people, yet many churchgoers and former churchgoers don't experience intellectual authenticity when it comes to difficult questions raised in church. Drew Dyck discovered the same complaint among people who have left the church. They "felt like Christians don't have an appreciation for the nuances of reality. . . . Christians offer easy answers to complex questions." Dyck gives his own honest evaluation to this complaint: "I don't think Christian are simplistic thinkers. But I think that sometimes we feel the need to project an ironclad certitude when talking about our faith."[7]

This ironclad certitude that leaves no room for discussion or disagreement is a common theme across David Kinnaman's survey of Millennials. Of his six descriptions of why Christian Millennials are turned off by church, at least three are relevant here: Christianity is *shallow, antiscience,* and *unwilling to wrestle with someone's doubts.* While Millennials are often accused of being lazy, selfish, immoral, or not wanting the truth (some of which accusations are certainly accurate), Kinnaman identifies a hunger in their souls that churches should be eager to feed:

This generation wants and needs truth, not spiritual soft-serve. According to our findings, churches too often provide lightweight teaching instead of rich knowledge that leads to wisdom. This is a generation hungry for substantive answers to life's biggest questions, particularly in a time when there are untold ways to access information about *what to do.* What's missing—and where the Christian community must come in—is addressing *how* and *why.*[8]

As a college professor, I wholeheartedly agree with Kinnaman. My students on the whole have deep questions about life, faith, sexuality, ethics, race, politics, immigration, justice, and a myriad of other topics that keep them up at night. And what makes my job so difficult is that they see right through thin answers to thick questions. Millennials are not like Gen-Xers and Boomers in this regard. When I was a college student back in the 1990s, I believed everything my professor said. After all, he's the professor! He must know what he's talking about. Boomers are even more hardwired to believe an older and wiser authority on any given topic. (Perhaps because they are usually the ones who are older and wiser . . .) But not so with Millennials. They have too much access to information and other "authorities" (including Wikipedia, unfortunately). They aren't satisfied with memorizing the right answer. They're wrestling with too many "right answers" floating around on the Internet. They want to know *why* and *how* and *why not.*

Translating Truths and Kingdom Ways

Life really does turn upside down in your twenties! For many, it is a season of deep soul searching and questioning. *What do I really want to give my life to? Does my vocation matter to God? Are there more "gray areas" than I used to think?*

There are indeed core, eternal truths about Jesus and his kingdom that make for a foundation in our daily lives. However, for young adults to continue in discipleship, they must translate these truths and kingdom ways to their new and different contexts— where they live, work, and play. They must have the mental discipline to press through hardship and disorienting changes, to "take captive every thought to make it obedient to Christ" (2 Corinthians 10:5, NIV). In the Nav20s, it is our purpose to help twenty-somethings to make this transition well, to know Christ and to make disciples of Christ for a lifetime.

CHAD SELJE, US Director of Nav20s

You know what's gained the most credibility with my students over the years? Shockingly, it's when I say, "I don't know." I used to fight against it. I thought that as the professor, I should always have all the answers all the time for all my students. But this became exhausting, especially since I only had some of the right answers to a few questions some of the time. Whenever I tried to cook up a "right answer" on the spot, they could see right through it. And they weren't impressed. Over the years I built up the courage to say, "You know what? I don't know the answer to your question. Why don't we think through it together?" And my professor points went through the roof.

Jesus' Teaching Method

Some of you may think that this is cowardly or unprofessional. Teachers need to give the answers, and students need to listen to them. And just to be clear, sometimes this is true. A professor who spends the majority of the class hour saying, "I don't know" should probably be fired. There are times when I say, "This is what the Bible says, and if you're a Christian, you'll believe it." But I still try to show them where, why, and how. After all, I don't want them just to believe me. I want them to see where it says this in the text and to be able to navigate a thoughtful conversation with those who disagree.

But what's fascinating is that even Jesus didn't usually take a heavy-handed, monological approach. Sometimes he gave a lecture, where he didn't take questions. The Sermon on the Mount (Matthew 5–7) and his scathing rebuke of the Scribes and Pharisees (Matthew 23) come to mind. But most of his interactions with people were just that: *interactions.*

For instance, Jesus interacted on a conversational level with the woman at the well and led her in the ways of truth through dialogue (John 4:1-26). He did the same with the disciples when they returned from the city and wondered why he was talking with a Samaritan woman (John 4:27-38). When the crowds met Jesus on the shores of the sea, he invited them to explore the nature of the kingdom by giving them a series of parables (Matthew 13:1-35). When an educated teacher of the law wanted to know how to have eternal life, Jesus told him a story about a good Samaritan and then asked a question: "Which of these three, do you think, proved to be a neighbor to the man who fell among the robbers?" (Luke 10:36).

Much of Jesus's teaching happened on a conversational level.[9] He stimulated people's thinking with questions, stories, parables, and analogies, and he led them to the truth without spoon-feeding it to them. I love how Greg Ogden puts it:

> Jesus allowed the disciples to live with conundrums. . . . No easy answers were provided, nor were there fill-in-the-blank workbooks. He wanted disciples who would have to think through the issues. Included in discipleship is the discipleship of the mind.[10]

Paul's famous encounter with the philosophers on Mars Hill looked the same. Although he ended with a monologue and a plea to repent (Acts 17:22-31), he got this opportunity because he spent several days engaging with them in dialogical conversations:

> He reasoned in the synagogue with the Jews and the devout persons, and in the marketplace every day with those who happened to be there. Some of the Epicurean and Stoic philosophers also conversed with him.
>
> ACTS 17:17-18

Many of today's discipleship methods are more monological than dialogical, and they don't provoke good critical thinking. As Greg Ogden says, "Too much of the material that is produced under the heading of discipleship curriculum is spoon-fed pabulum. Jesus intentionally troubled the disciples by challenging their cherished assumptions."[11]

Learning in the Early Church

The early church was devoted to learning. One could not say, "I want to be a Christian" and then say, "But I just want to love Jesus and not use my mind." The two went hand in hand. When someone got saved during the early church period (AD 100–500), they were required to go through *three years* of intense study of the Bible and Christian theology.[12] I'm not talking about aspiring pastors or missionaries. I'm talking about *all Christians.* The early church didn't think learning was an option. To be a Christian was to be a critical thinker.

And this has been true for most of Christian tradition. Until recently, Christians were always leading the way in the study of science, art, philosophy, literature, and various other subjects. Christians were the ones who invented the very concept of a university, where all subjects could be explored and mastered. The word *university* itself comes from two Latin words: *uni* and *veritas,* which mean "one truth." In other words, there is one Christian truth that binds together and interprets all other truths in the world. Christianity has always been passionate about critical thinking. It's never settled for memorizing certain doctrines and then just sticking our fingers in our ears and saying, "La la la la" to all of the hard questions the world throws our way.

Christianity has always been passionate about critical thinking.

The anti-intellectual, biblically illiterate, indoctrinating form of discipleship that plagues the church is stifling true, holistic spiritual growth.

Thoughtful Dialogue as Discipleship

The church needs to be a safe place to dialogue. We can't be scared of hard questions, and we need to stop giving prepackaged, canned responses to complex issues. As we saw above, one of the biggest complaints about Christians, especially from younger people, is that we are too scared or ill-equipped to think through the tough questions of the day. We love to hear ourselves talk, and we keep regurgitating dogmatic answers to complex questions. We're not known for thoughtfully and honestly engaging topics that matter. And many people are fleeing our churches because of it.

As I am writing this book, I'm also writing a series of blogs wrestling with a Christian theology of "intersex."[13] Intersex persons are born with ambiguous genitalia, or a combination of both male and female biological characteristics. Some are even born with male XY chromosomes but female genitalia. Are they male? Female? Or some sort of sexual "other"? Are male and female the only two sexual categories, or do intersex persons show that there are other options? Did God make intersex persons this way? If marriage is between a man and woman, then whom should an intersex person marry? What if the doctor who "fixed" the deformity cut off the wrong part, and the female baby shows himself to actually be a boy later on in life?

How would you respond to these questions? Some would

respond: "All humans are either male are female—period! La la la la la la." But there's a better response that appreciates the complexity of the questions, while revisiting God's Word in humble dialogue with others doing the same.

There are many issues in life that require good, hard, honest, intelligent discussion. Should Christians fight against gun control? Is euthanasia always ethically wrong? How do we know that life begins at conception? Why are same-sex relations sin? *Are* they sin? Should we destroy our enemies or love them? Is ISIS our enemy?

Maybe there's a "right answer" to all of these, but maybe there's some gray area that will take some time to explore. Maybe we'll go to the grave not having figured everything out, and that's okay. The point is to engage the critical questions in life with honesty and Christian care and, above all, to not demonize people for asking hard questions.

As I was blogging about the intersex topic, the most common response I got from people was, "Thank you for taking the time to talk about this. I've been wrestling with this question for a while, yet no one in my church is wiling (or able) to talk about it." Part of discipleship is helping people think through the critical issues of the day—helping them to be transformed by the renewal of their minds (Romans 12:2) and to "take every thought captive to obey Christ" (2 Corinthians 10:5). After all, Jesus commanded us to "love the Lord your God with all your heart and with all your soul and with your *mind*" (Matthew 22:37, emphasis added). Loving God with our minds can't happen if we leave our minds in the foyer as we walk into church.

Creating Safe Environments for Honest Dialogue

So how can we train Christians to think well as part of their discipleship? The most effective way I've found is to create safe and thoughtful environments for honest dialogue. In other words, we can't rely on Sunday sermons to cultivate a biblical worldview among the people. There must be more.

Think about it. The fact is, most Sunday services are monological. They involve one person talking to many. Have you ever had questions about a sermon? Miscellaneous thoughts? Disagreements? Did you ever wish you could stop and ask for clarification or go deeper into a particular point?

I believe there's a place for monological teaching. I don't think we should do away with Sunday-morning sermons. However, younger people especially are growing up in a world of blogs and online news articles and interactive websites and YouTube videos. They can always ask questions or make comments. Personally, I find most of these comments quite annoying, and you probably do too. (If you don't think they're annoying, you might be the one commenting too much . . .) But annoying or not, that's the world we live in. So it does feel a bit odd for many people to listen to a sermon and not have any space to dialogue about it.

Pastor and author Dan Kimball asked a bunch of people what they wished church was like. The response he got confirms my suspicion.

Virtually the first thing every single person I talked to said is that they wish church weren't just a sermon but a discussion. They uniformly expressed that they do not want to only sit and listen to a preacher giving a lecture. And it's not because they don't want to learn. They expressed a strong desire to learn the teachings of Jesus and to learn about the Bible. Rather, they feel they can learn better if they can participate and ask questions.[14]

Some churches create such space by devoting post-sermon time for Q & A. Small churches are more conducive to live Q & A, but larger churches usually take questions via text. Other churches offer a postservice gathering that's devoted to discussion. Now, this may not catch on. After all, many Christians are preprogrammed to come, listen, try to stay awake, and then rush home. But what would Jesus do? I think he would work hard to deprogram people, to wean them off of their religious routine. He'd challenge their assumptions and awaken their minds so they could learn to love God with heart and head.

Sunday-morning services may not be the best place for dialogue, or at least they shouldn't be the only place. Genuine dialogue and interaction are best fostered in smaller settings. While one-on-one relations can be great for focused discussion and learning, I still think that a group of three to ten people can cultivate a healthy array of different perspectives and questions. I don't mean this to be legalistic; there's no magic number. But over the years I've seen more and more people shut down as the group gets larger. In my classes, about 20 percent of the students do 90 percent of the talking. In smaller groups, a much higher percentage of people will be more prone to interact.

You can also create other spaces outside the traditional

Sunday service and midweek group. When it comes to learning and dialogue, the possibilities are endless. You could devote a special night (weekly, monthly, or bimonthly) to teaching and discussing hard topics. Or what about quarterly or yearly seminars or mini-conferences that are devoted to engaging with the ideas that everyone is already thinking about (politics, sex, money, terrorism, sex, race, sex, money)?

In Boise, where I live, I recently teamed up with a local pastor and another Christian leader to host what we call "City Forums." These forums are monthly public dialogues on topics that live at the intersection of faith and culture. We want to talk publicly about stuff that everyone—not just the church—is talking about. An expert in a particular area gives a forty-five-minute talk, followed by another forty-five minutes of dialogue. (It often turns into a two-hour dialogue!) We just sort of drummed up the idea one day and decided to go for it. I planned to give the first talk on "homosexuality and the church," since we wanted to start off with a nice, easy, noncontroversial subject. (What was I thinking?) We had no idea how it would go. As it turned out, more than one hundred people showed up. Most were Christians from about twenty different churches in the area. Others were non-Christians who heard about the event through the grapevine or through a Christian friend. Most were straight; some were gay. And everyone, I believe, felt safe to ask really hard questions and even disagree with the speaker—which wasn't easy but was tremendously rewarding.

Notice that the City Forums aren't just a free-for-all, where everyone could toss out their opinions and go home feeling good about their views. In order to honor the truth of God's Word, we have an expert who has a biblical world-view address each topic. But in order to foster education rather than indoctrination, we created a safe space for people to ask questions and dialogue with the speaker and with each other.

Here's the thing: the City Forums aren't something separate from discipleship. Rather, the forums are one of many ways in which the church can help its people sharpen their thinking through learning, discussing, questioning, and being able to ask those hard questions that they've been so scared to bring up in church.

I don't want to go too far down the rabbit hole of method. I'm not saying that every service must take text questions or that you, too, need to start your own City Forums. The point is that we need to think intentionally about how we can create safe places for people to ask hard questions and receive thoughtful answers. This is not icing on the cake of discipleship. It's not an optional deluxe package to an other-wise fine-running car. It's part of the engine itself.

Discipleship without learning is not biblical discipleship.

MISSION: NOT JUST MORALITY

In September 2015, my wife and I had the chance to visit the French Quarter of New Orleans for the first time. My friend Tom Bilderback pastors Vieux Carre Baptist Church, smack dab in the middle of the French Quarter. To the locals, it's just known as "the Vieux" (it's French, so don't pronounce the "x").

Tom and his wife, Sonia, invited me to come down, to give a few talks to his leaders, and to preach on Sunday morning. My wife and I were so excited! A chance to get away and stroll around this historic city, listening to jazz musicians play "When the Saints Go Marching In" as parents drank sweet tea while kids played in the streets.

My expectations were crushed. The Vieux meets one

block off Bourbon Street in the French Quarter—basically a modern-day Sodom and Gomorrah. Bourbon Street is what you get when you sear a human conscience, pump it full of alcohol, crank up the music, and take away all law and moral restraint. It's not uncommon for two drunk people to have sex in the street, puke their guts out, pass out unconscious on the sidewalk, wake up to defecate, and then drift back into an alcoholic slumber—all before noon. Let's just say that my visions of sipping sweet tea on Colonel Sanders's front porch didn't come true.

But I saw Jesus. He lives right off Bourbon Street. He resides in the embodied love and grace of a radical little group of Christian misfits who call themselves The Vieux. I was blown away at the power of Jesus at work in this community. People are getting saved. Drunks are coming to Christ. And homeless people are finding family in a ragtag group of Jesus followers who have left comfort and security to live on mission in a godless city.

Over the weekend, I met several people who spent most of their lives on the streets sucking on a bottle of liquor. Yet they have found Jesus and now are serving him with reckless abandon. These are genuine converts—real Jesus followers. Like "Mamma Rose," as she's known by everyone in the Quarter. Mamma spent a good forty to fifty years of her life on the streets, downing two liters of vodka a day. I did the math: that's equivalent to forty beers a day. I don't think Mamma was sober for more than an hour since the early 1980s. Previous pastors of the Vieux reached out to her, and Tom and Sonia picked up where they left off. They befriended her, helped her, and built a relationship with her—something that the angry street preachers who parachute into the Quarter on Saturday nights to yell at the drunks would never do. She's been clean now for a couple years, and she's telling everyone about Jesus.

Then there's Jim, who has been divorced three times and spent most of his life on the streets of the French Quarter nursing an addiction to drugs and alcohol. Pastor Tom reached out to him with the love of Christ. Now Jim's a leader in the church. Jim's one of the kindest, most grateful Christians I've ever met. And talk about brilliant: Jim studied to be a tour guide in the Quarter, and now knows everything there is to know about its history.

Story after story, convert after convert, I became addicted to hearing about the love of Christ that overflows the walls of The Vieux and spills into the streets of Sodom. The life of these disciples gave me life. Their sacrifice challenged my comfort. And I was reminded once again of the power of mission-centered, grace-filled discipleship when Christ followers take it to the streets.

More Than Morality

Discipleship is far more than just mastering morality. It's even more than thinking critically about tough topics, despite my plea in the previous chapter. Biblical discipleship must include mission—embodying and displaying the presence of Christ beyond the four walls of church.

What I love about the ministry at the Vieux is that there was no clear distinction between discipleship and non-discipleship activities. The complaint among pastors that people only spend three hours a week pursuing spiritual growth wouldn't make sense at The Vieux. If you ask Mamma Rose how many hours she spends pursuing spiritual growth, she'd probably laugh and say, "Every minute that I'm not sucking on a bottle." Tom, Sonia, and the other leaders at The Vieux are living out their discipleship the second they get within a mile of church. Whether it's providing a meal and a shower for the homeless on Friday nights, or praying over people as they walk from church to dinner (a daily scene), there's never a time when the discipleship light turns off and then back on. The city on a hill is always lit.

Remember: to be a Christian is to be a disciple. And to be a disciple is to be on mission.

While Jesus went to synagogue and visited the Temple on occasion, his primary mode of discipleship was mission. By mission I mean spreading the Good News of the gospel through proclamation, love, and service. Or as Brandon Hatmaker says: "It's good news when we speak the gospel message . . . and it's good news when we live incarnationally and take on the posture of Christ to others, humbly serving them."[1] Being on mission means both talking about the love of Christ and demonstrating the love of Christ. The mission includes telling others about Jesus, calling people to faith and repentance, and teaching them about the story of God. But being on mission goes beyond the words that we speak; it includes loving people with our hands and feet as tangible displays of the love of Christ. Incarnation and proclamation go hand in hand.

Living Missionally

In a large city like New York we always hear about people who get "lost" in their work, want to "be" in the right social happenings, get "caught up" in a community cause, or just "lose" themselves in any number of things. After all, "you only live once" (YOLO), which carries the "fear of missing out" (FOMO). Were it not for the faithful followers of Jesus living their lives suspiciously different yet attractively inviting, many people would be lost and without hope.

These are the people who cheerfully greet you each morning as you get your morning coffee. They are the ones who treat you with the same deference whether you are a "nobody" or a "somebody". They set the work standard of excellence, integrity, and teaming. They are the ones you want to be around. When the world is crashing down, they have joy and peace, for they are not of this world. They provide light in darkness. They are the fragrance and aroma of Christ that permeates all of life. Their lives are attractive, and they make a difference in their work. They affect the workplace, the city, and beyond.

AL MIYASHITA, mission director, NavWorkplace

This is why Jesus touched and loved and healed lost sinners in a dying world. Sometimes his love led to faith and conversion, while other times it led to rejection. Either way, the Good News was being proclaimed through word and deed.

The parable of the Good Samaritan is a classic example

of being on mission. The Samaritan wasn't on a "mission trip." He wasn't clocked in to do some ministry. He was just going about his daily business and saw a man in need. He gave of his time and money to extend neighborly love to a man he didn't know. Maybe the man in the ditch was a good man. Maybe he was not. Maybe he was a tax collector or rabbi, a sex offender or pastor. The Samaritan didn't know. He didn't care. Here was a human in need, and his impulse to love his neighbor kicked in.

We don't know if the man "got saved" through the Samaritan's actions. That's not the point of the story. The point is that followers of Jesus must demonstrate love for all people as an extension of Christ's love for the world.

The early Christians integrated this posture into their daily lives. Peter and John were going about their business when they converted and healed a lame beggar. Stephen was going about his business when he was arrested and gave his final testimony before he was killed. Philip was going about his business when the Spirit of God directed him to an Ethiopian eunuch. Ananias was going about his business when God called on him to convert and baptize Paul, the persecutor of the church.

The first Christians didn't just send out missionaries. They were missionaries.

The first Christians didn't just send out missionaries. They were missionaries.

Our ultimate desire, of course, is that everyone would come to the saving knowledge of Christ (see 2 Peter 3:9). But our love and service is not conditioned upon conversion. We don't just extend love *so that* people get saved but *because* God's love is boundless and showers down upon all (Matthew 5:44-46).[2]

Being on mission means embodying the loving and convicting presence of Christ to the world around us. You don't need to fly over salt water to engage the mission; embodying Christ's love is something all disciples should do. This mission is fundamental to who we are as Christians and disciples, and therefore it's an essential piece of the church's discipleship.

Holy Longing

Even though "mission" is central to discipleship, it's often not included in the church's repertoire of discipleship activities. Most of the discipleship activities (Sunday school, Bible studies, and so on) focus on teaching and learning. Or they focus on Christians hanging out with other Christians and getting to know each other better. And both of these are good! I've argued in previous chapters that teaching/learning and fellowship/community are essential components of discipleship. However, they are still incomplete without mission.

One of the reasons why mission is so important—aside from the fact that it's biblical—is that people are actually hungry for it. When Packard and Hope interviewed all of their "church refugees," they were shocked that these church dropouts were once some of the most active members in church.

> Almost without exception, our respondents were deeply involved and devoted to their churches up until the moment they left. They were integrated into leadership structures and church life, often organizing daily life around the church and

attending some kind of church function two or
more times a week. They're the kind of people
who are drawn to activity.[3]

If they were so committed, so active, and so engaged, why
did they leave? The answer is rather sad. It makes me feel
frustrated yet hopeful at the same time. "Nearly all of our
respondents wanted . . . the church to leverage its organiza-
tional resources and infrastructure to get more things done
outside of the church walls and to build community."[4]

There are so many people in church and outside church
who passionately desire to engage in meaningful activity: con-
fronting poverty, fighting injustice, doing good for the community, and reaching the lost with tangible love and the Good
News of Jesus Christ. Even people outside the church are
looking to do something meaningful. According to a recent
Barna study, many unchurched adults are seekers, and 80 percent say they care deeply about social justice.[5] What a massive
bridge for the gospel! Jesus cares about social justice too.

David Kinnaman shares a sad story about a church dropout named Tracy. Though raised in the church, she became
disillusioned with Christianity and ended up fading away
from the faith. However, she always had a passion to help
the poor. She spent some time in Tanzania to work with
vulnerable people. After hearing her story and her heart
for the vulnerable, Kinnaman said to her in passing, "It
seems like God has put it in your heart. You were made for
it." After all, Tracy's heart for the poor echoes God's heart
(Matthew 25:31-46). Her response was disheartening: "Oh,
huh. I never thought of my interest in helping the poor

around the world as a calling from God. It just feels like in America everyone keeps faith separate from work and life."[6]

How is it that someone can grow up in church and cultivate a passion for the poor and vulnerable yet never be shown—discipled—how this is deeply connected to the heart of Christ? And this isn't just an isolated incident. Only 20 percent of Millennials who grew up in church say that they had opportunities to serve the poor through their church. Even fewer (15 percent) said they found a cause or issue at church that motivated them.[7]

Several churches I know are recognizing this incessant, God-given, Jesus-reflecting desire to serve the poor and the community, and they have integrated some sort of "Serve Sunday" into their church calendar. One awesome church in Boise cancels the church service every six weeks in order to go out into the community and physically serve others around them.[8] They partner with several nonprofit organizations in town and ask them, "How can we serve you?" Sometimes it's picking weeds at a women's halfway house, or maybe it's helping out at a garden that provides food for refugees. Whatever it is, their heart is to bring the tangible love of Christ to bear on the community through real acts of physical service.

Rather than just doing church work, they're doing the work of the church.[9]

You know what's interesting? The pastor told me that these "Serve Sundays" are usually the most well-attended Sundays of the month! At first I was shocked. I thought that if you "canceled church" (which isn't a theologically correct description of what's going on), hardly anyone would show up. But the opposite is true. Deep down in the heart of most people is a desire to engage in meaningful activity.

What's even more fascinating is that most members of this church find it much easier to bring their friends to this type of "service." After all, it's not just Christians who seek the good of their community. When unbelievers find out that Christians actually care about the real needs around them, they usually perk up and want to listen to what we have to say.

Most Christians (and many non-Christians) desire to do good in their community. They want to serve the poor, confront injustice, combat racism, help refugees, and share the love of Christ through word and deed—especially deed. Part of our discipleship process should empower people to engage the mission of Christ wherever they are.

We shouldn't see discipleship activities like church services and Bible studies as preparation for the mission. Jesus didn't take this approach and neither should we. Rather, we should view missional activities as part of the discipleship journey. We learn, we serve, and we learn by serving.

Who's Doing This?

Mission is not something that occurs after disciples become mature. It's part of the maturation process of discipleship. Churches that desire to help disciples "be transformed into Christlikeness" need to integrate missional activities—or let's just call it a "missional lifestyle"—into its process.

I love what my friends at Imago Dei Church in Portland do to integrate mission into discipleship. They intentionally devote a significant part of their money to help fund missional projects that are created and developed by members of the church. They call them "missional grants." Not every project gets funded. There's a whole application and interview process that identifies the most promising ideas. But every year, the church gives anywhere from $100,000 to $200,000 toward missional projects that are designed to further God's kingdom in Portland.

I love this idea for several reasons. First, it allocates some church funds toward local missions. Too many church budgets are sucked up by Sunday services, and not enough is given toward discipleship and missions. And quite frankly, many Christians are getting tired of it. They want to see more funds allocated toward meaningful and missional ventures. When Imago Dei funds such missional projects, it shows that they care about extending Christ's love beyond the four walls of church. This resonates with its people—and with Jesus as well.

Second, by funding these projects, Imago Dei empowers the people. Remember the asset-based community development (ABCD) principles from chapter 5? As image bearers, all people possess gifts and talents that should be used to further God's kingdom. Yet people often feel stifled or forced to fit into a few prepackaged programs that are created from the top down. By funding projects created by the people, Imago Dei empowers and encourages people to explore their own passions for God's kingdom. My friend Joshua Ryan Butler, the outreach pastor at Imago Dei, says it like this:

> We have an unwritten rule at our church: "pastors can't start ministries." When people hear this, they're often shocked, like "But isn't that your job? The Outreach Pastor to start ministries and get people

into them?" But we start from the opposite end: we believe God has gifted his people, the body of Christ, with vision, talent, and imagination—they have better ideas than I do! And that's a good thing. So I see my role as the pastor not being to create the thing and rope them into it, but rather being available to help surface, equip, and unleash them in areas God might be calling them into—and then to shepherd them as they lead our church into embodying the love of Christ in those areas of our city.[10]

I mentioned my friend Shawn Gordon, who was discipled by Francis Chan. Shawn now helps run Project Bayview, a discipleship ministry where several men, mostly ex-cons like Shawn, live together above a restaurant.[11] Not only does the restaurant serve up some killer Hawaiian BBQ, but it also becomes a holistic discipleship center, where men cook, clean, work the counter, serve tables, and learn how to integrate the gospel into a workday. Above the restaurant, each disciple is paired up with a discipler. They live together, study together, pray together, and work together. When they're not studying the Bible or working in the restaurant, they're on the streets sharing the Good News of Jesus in a neighborhood where his love is greatly needed.

What if churches around the country created their own Project Bayviews, not as some nonprofit that they support from a distance but as an integral part of church life? My guess is that there would be a long waiting list of people wanting to help out with this ministry. Perhaps they'd have to start another Project Bayview . . . and another.

We need to stop thinking about mission as some subsidiary part of our church experience, which usually focuses on Sunday services. When mission becomes more central, discipleship becomes more tangible and effective.

When mission becomes more central, discipleship becomes more tangible and effective.

I recently read Brandon Hatmaker's book *Barefoot Church* just before Brandon and I hung out on a hunting trip in Montana. I can't remember whether I read about his story in his book, or if I got it from our campfire conversations. Anyway, it's a challenging testimony that made me think, *I want to do that!*

Brandon was on staff at a megachurch in Texas—living the pastoral dream. But God started to wreck his life by telling him to serve the poor. So Brandon dragged his grill downtown to where the homeless would hang out, and he started barbecuing burgers as an avenue for relationship. Over the next few weeks, more and more people came to hang out and talk about life, love, community, and Jesus. Brandon told me that he hit a turning point in his "grilling sessions" when an unchurched, agnostic woman was on the grill cooking for the masses. Someone blurted out, "What if church was kind of like this?" Without lifting up her head, the woman said, "If church was like this, *I would go to that church.*" She kept on grilling. Brandon realized he wasn't just grilling burgers and hanging out with the homeless. He was planting a church.

Brandon followed Jesus all the way to the poor, and a church sprang up. If that's not discipleship, I don't know what is. Mission and discipleship belong together. You can't have one without the other.

Missional Living

Just to be clear, despite everything I've said in this chapter, I don't believe we should replace morality with mission. To become like Jesus, we need to pursue sexual purity, sobriety, generosity, selflessness, and kindness, and we need to put to death personal vices such as anger, greed, jealousy, lust, and pride. My point is not to replace morality with mission but to view mission as part of morality.

I want to close this chapter by giving a more thorough description of what it means to live missionally. I just so happened to stumble upon a description of the term *missional* in Dan Kimball's book *They Like Jesus but Not the Church*. It's honestly the best summary I think I've ever seen. So instead of reinventing the wheel, I'll just hijack Dan's description—giving him full credit, of course:[12]

- Being missional means that the church sees itself as *being* missionaries, rather than having a missions department, and that we see ourselves as missionaries right where we live.
- Being missional means that we see ourselves as representatives of Jesus "sent" into our communities, and that the church aligns everything it does with the *missio Dei* (mission of God).
- Being missional means we see the church not as a place we go only on Sunday but as something we are throughout the week.
- Being missional means that we understand we don't "bring Jesus" to people but that we realize Jesus is active in culture and we join him in what he is doing.

- Being missional means we are very much in the world and engaged in culture but are not conforming to the world.
- Being missional means we serve our communities and that we build relationships with the people in them, rather than seeing them as evangelistic targets.
- Being missional means being all the more dependent on Jesus and the Spirit through prayer, the Scriptures, and each other in community.

8

THE MOST SEGREGATED HOUR
OF THE WEEK

For most of my Christian life, I've attended churches that were filled with middle-class (or wealthy) white people. I never really thought much of it. After all, I'm white, and like-minded people of the same race or ethnicity seem to naturally get along better. Why prevent a good thing? If a church happens to grow into one, big, ethnically homogeneous machine, then more power to them.

Sure, it's kind of cool if people of different ethnicities join the same church. It might be good to have young people worshiping with older people. Perhaps it can be neat if rich people are in community with poor people. But none of this is necessary. As long as a church is growing, as long as disciples are being made, the diversity of the growth is largely irrelevant.

This is how I used to think. But then I reread the Bible. And I discovered that my thinking was wrong.

American evangelical churches are largely homogeneous. They're packed with people who for the most part look the same, act the same, and smell the same. According to sociologist Michael Emerson, only 13.7 percent of American churches are multiethnic, where no ethnicity makes up more than 80 percent of its members.[1] This means that the church is one of the most segregated institutions in America. Long after the civil rights movement, Sunday morning still remains the most segregated time in America.[2] What's striking is that most Christians don't really care. Sixty-seven percent of churchgoers "say their church has done enough to become racially diverse. And less than half think their church should become more diverse."[3]

Now let me be frank. *If* ethnic segregation is irrelevant to the gospel—if Jesus is standing in heaven, arms folded, looking down at all our segregated churches and thinking, *Now there's a job well done*—then the church's segregation doesn't matter. But if God actually desires all types of people to worship together and follow Jesus together and be reconciled to each other, then we have a serious problem on our hands. And here's the thing: *Our lack of diversity is hindering our discipleship.*

The Vocabulary of Diversity

Before we go further, let's define a few terms and ideas.

First, *race* and *ethnicity*. Although people use these terms interchangeably, it's important to understand the difference. *Race* is a biological term that refers to one's physical characteristics, such as bone structure and skin color. *Ethnicity* is a sociological term that describes one's nationality, regional culture, language, and other features that go beyond one's biology. For the sake of our discussion, I want to talk primarily about *ethnic* diversity rather than *racial* diversity. Ethnicity is a more holistic concept and includes race but isn't limited to race. Plus, it's biblical. The Bible doesn't talk about different races but different ethnicities—ethnicities that are reconciled to each other through the gospel (Genesis 12:3; Galatians 3:8; Ephesians 2:14-16).

The second set of terms we need to understand is *diversity* versus *reconciliation.*[4] Although diversity is a beautiful thing and the start of an even better thing, it's not the end goal. I'm not arguing for simply cramming a bunch of different ethnicities together into a shared space and saying, "Well done, good and faithful servants." Any sort of affirmative-action program or non-governmental organization can accomplish that. But only Jesus can accomplish ethnic *reconciliation*—tearing down walls of division and animosity and forming a unified body of Jesus followers. Forming diverse communities is a good start. But it's only a start. The gospel that Jesus and Paul preached was a gospel of *reconciliation* (2 Corinthians 5:11-21).

Lastly, *assimilation* versus *integration.* Assimilation happens when a minority group joins a majority group and simply absorbs into the majority group. One of my friends joked about his dad who talked "positively" about the black couple (there was only one) in their church. "I'm not racist," he said. "In fact, I love the Smiths. They're so great, you'd hardly even know they're black."

If you don't know why that statement is funny or scary, then please keep reading this chapter. What we don't want to see is one dominant group, whether white or rich or poor or black, that swallows up all minority groups into their culture. We don't want minority groups to *assimilate* into a majority group; rather, we want all beautifully diverse people to *integrate* into one composite whole, where God's manifold glory is refracted through a diverse group of image bearers united and reconciled through the gospel.[5]

Before you conclude that this is all some liberal tangent, let's do what we've been doing throughout this book. Let's see what Scripture says about the multicultural Good News of Jesus.[6]

The Multicolored Gospel

The gospel of Jesus Christ was focused, in part, on bringing about unity and reconciliation to a diverse group of people. Paul could not have said this more clearly than he did in Ephesians 2:14-16:

> For he himself is our peace, who has made us
> both one and has broken down in his flesh the
> dividing wall of hostility by abolishing the law of
> commandments expressed in ordinances, that he
> might create in himself one new man in place of
> the two, so making peace, and might reconcile
> us both to God in one body through the cross,
> thereby killing the hostility.

Speaking to Gentiles, Paul says that Jesus died to tear down the dividing wall of hostility that separated them from the

Jews. In the first century, the Jews divided humanity into two groups of people: Jews and Gentiles. Paul's statement in Ephesians 2 is all about ethnic reconciliation. The "one new man in place of the two," which describes the church God intends to build through the blood of Christ, is a multicultural phenomenon.

Notice we're not just talking about *diversity*. We're talking about blood-bought *reconciliation*. We're also not talking about doing away with ethnicities but crushing the animosity that divides us. Multiethnicity is good. Division between ethnicities is bad. Put simply, the Cross intends to do away with uniculturalism and to create multicultural communities.

Paul continues this same theme in Ephesians 3 when he talks about his apostolic ministry to the Gentiles:

> Though I am the least deserving of all God's people, he graciously gave me the privilege of telling the Gentiles about the endless treasures available to them in Christ. I was chosen to explain to everyone this mysterious plan that God, the Creator of all things, had kept secret from the beginning. *God's purpose in all this was to use the church to display his wisdom in its rich variety to all the unseen rulers and authorities in the heavenly places.* This was his eternal plan, which he carried out through Christ Jesus our Lord.
>
> EPHESIANS 3:8-11, NLT, EMPHASIS ADDED

This passage deserves a slow reading. Linger on it a bit, especially verse 10. It's the climax of the entire chapter. In the context of bringing two ethnic groups together—Jew and

Gentile—Paul says that their unity as one church displays God's "wisdom in its rich variety to all the unseen rulers and authorities." Think about that: Ethnically diverse, spiritually unified, Christ-exalting churches declare to Satan and his minions, *You lost!*

Ethnically diverse, spiritually unified, Christ-exalting churches declare to Satan and his minions, You lost!

Paul calls ethnic disunity a gospel issue in Galatians 2, when he confronts Peter for not eating with Gentiles—a sign of division rather than reconciliation. Paul tells Peter that he was "not in step with *the truth of the gospel*" (Galatians 2:14, emphasis added).

Paul didn't say, "Peter, you really should be more inclusive of other ethnic groups. But this isn't a gospel issue, so don't worry too much about it." Rather, Paul confronts Peter for violating the "truth of the gospel" by rebuilding the ethnic walls that Jesus already tore down.

Breaking down ethnic barriers is not an optional add-on to the gospel. It's intrinsic to the good news that Jesus is the Savior of all.

Jesus often challenged racism (or ethnocentrism)[7] and segregation—probably more often than you think. He reached out to several Samaritans, something unheard-of in his Jewish community. He loved Canaanites, Romans, and other Gentiles who were deemed unclean and inherently sinful by other religious leaders. None of this was coincidence. All of it was intentional. Jesus was fulfilling God's original promise to include "all the families of the earth" in his covenant family (Genesis 12:3). A God whose image is reflected and refracted through every ethnicity can best be represented on earth by an ethnically diverse community.

The early Christians also sought to build a multiethnic representation of God. Throughout the book of Acts, we see every tribe and every nation coming to worship King Jesus in unison (Acts 2:8-11; 8:4-8, 26-40). One of the most influential churches in Acts was the church at Antioch. It was led by a multicultural team of prophets and teachers, which included two Africans (Lucius and Simeon), two Middle Eastern Jews, and a Jew from Asia Minor named Saul (Acts 13:1). The early church was one big messy melting pot of ethnic diversity gathered in unity around a multicultural God.

It wasn't easy. One of the first major disputes in the church had to do with ethnic tension (Acts 6:1-6). But the early Christians believed that tearing down ethnic barriers is part of the mission that God sent them on when they were commissioned to make disciples of all nations (Matthew 28:18-20).

Other Forms of Diversity

Gender diversity is another key component of reflecting God's diverse image. "God created man in his own image, in the image of God he created him; *male and female* he created them" (Genesis 1:27, emphasis added). This statement was revolutionary in the ancient world, where men were viewed as superior to women. According to God, both men and women equally and beautifully reflect God's image. If you visit a monastery or a convent, you'll get an incomplete image of God, because God is best displayed through both males *and* females.

When I was on the preaching team at Cornerstone Church in California, we realized that our preaching meetings (where we'd get together and talk through the upcoming message) had only men, even though more than half of the people we were preaching to were women. So we invited a woman into the group. It was one of the most eye-opening things I've ever experienced. As we would run illustrations and interpretations by her, she would tell us how these would be heard by a woman. All of us guys would sit back and realize in bewilderment how we have never taken the time to put ourselves in the shoes of the women listening to our sermons.

We need to make sure that women don't feel undervalued, underappreciated, or nonessential for the mission of the church. Gender reconciliation is part of discipleship.[8]

Diversity and reconciliation as a discipleship priority extends to age and socioeconomic status as well. There is no place for power differentials in a gathering of believers because God's people are characterized not by power or wealth or status but by our common allegiance to Jesus. When the world peers in on our gatherings and sees beggars and bankers joining arms in worship, they're forced to ask, *Why?* What caused this? What—or who—is bringing this about? Few things display the gospel more brilliantly than seeing the power of the Spirit and the Cross of Christ binding together radically different people who have no worldly business hanging out with each other.

Jesus knew this, which is why he gathered a comically diverse group of people. Rich business owners (James and John), violent revolutionaries (Simon), shady sellouts (Matthew), children, wealthy women (Mary, Joanna, and others in Luke 8:1-3), moral women, immoral women, beggars, blind people, crippled people, Roman soldiers, and those who wanted to kill Roman soldiers. The collage of misfits and moralists who flocked around Jesus turned a few heads and ruined his reputation (Matthew 11:19). This was the church Jesus was building, against which the gates of hell could not prevail.

I love the victorious declaration of Christ's finished work on the cross in Revelation 5:9-10 (NLT):

> You are worthy to take the scroll
>> and break its seals and open it.
> For you were slaughtered, and your blood has
>> ransomed people for God
>> from every tribe and language and people
>>> and nation.
> And you have caused them to become
>> a Kingdom of priests for our God.
>> And they will reign on the earth.

Segregated churches do not reflect the final goal of Christ's finished work according to Revelation 5. God never set out to redeem a bunch of white people or black people, rich people or poor people. Intrinsic to God's plan of redemption is to "ransom people for God *from every tribe and language and people and nation*" so that we will become "a Kingdom of priests for our God" and reign—together—"on the earth." It's a beautiful thing—indeed a gospel thing—when local churches display this global truth.

Diversity, Reconciliation, and Discipleship

It's one thing to affirm gospel-centered reconciliation. But this is a book about discipleship—becoming more like

135

Christ. We need to get beyond just affirming a truth; we need to put it into practice. So let's explore the different ways in which diversity and reconciliation fosters discipleship.

The first way is a simple one—since discipleship is becoming more like Jesus, and since Jesus formed diverse communities, then to be faithful disciples we should do what Jesus did. We should help build and participate in diverse communities so that gospel-centered and gospel-mandated reconciliation can take place. We should pursue the types of communities that Jesus did, communities that were anything but homogeneous.

Becoming like Jesus means we surround ourselves with diverse people. We become catalysts for ethnic reconciliation. We weed out racist subtleties in our hearts and address them when we see them in others. We welcome the stranger, the poor, the lame, the marginalized, the rich, the Gentile, the Jew into our homes and our lives. We value, humanize, learn from, submit to, and love people from every tribe, tongue, nation, and people. Following Jesus means we do what Jesus did and live the way he told us to live.

Second, we experience God through other people, especially a diverse group of people. In chapter 4 we saw how God is most fully experienced in community rather than on our own. Or in the words of Paul, "the church . . . is his body, the fullness of him who fills all in all" (Ephesians 1:22-23). The "fullness of" God inhabits other believers.

While God is experienced through other believers, he's most fully experienced through a diverse group of believers. This is why God is on a mission to reach all nations for Christ. God wants to create a manifold witness to his name on earth. And the diverse complexity of God is best displayed and experienced through a diverse group of image bearers.

Unity amid Diversity

At the heart of every Navigator is a burning desire to know Christ and to make him known. Unity amid diversity is vital in seeing this passion fulfilled. Jesus says in John 17:23 (NIV), "I in them and you in me—so that they may be brought to complete unity. Then the world will know that you sent me."

In Jesus words we see that unity comes through the indwelling relationship we each have with Christ. It is also that unity which makes Christ known to the world!

Our aim in The Navigators is not assimilation or some form of "melting pot," but rather a unity amidst diversity where each race, ethnicity, and culture brings its own contribution into our common desire to know Christ and make him known. Through unity amid diversity we each grow in our knowledge of God, and we help each other make him known to a watching world.

No one race, ethnicity, or culture alone is large enough for this task.

STEVE SHANK, director, Navigators Strategic Initiatives Office

---

Women mirror God in ways that men often don't, which is why Scripture sometimes uses female imagery to describe God.[9] Men display God's presence in different ways as well. Since God is not American or Canadian or Latino or Asian or African, we experience God best through a multiethnic community. If you want to engage the full, variegated, complex, and beautiful character of our Creator, then become part of a diverse Christian community and you'll be blessed. And challenged. And changed.

Third, we understand God better—and can therefore live more like God—when we learn from and listen to a diverse group of people. The fact is, our ethnicity, gender, age, and socioeconomic status all shape the way we view God. Take our reading of Scripture, for instance. I'll never forget the first time I noticed that every single deliverer in Exodus 1–4 was a woman. The Hebrew *midwives* rescued the firstborn males from being killed by Pharaoh. Then Moses' *mother* saved Moses by placing him in a basket. Pharaoh's *daughter* rescued Moses from the Nile River. Moses' *sister* Miriam continued to save Moses by allowing him to be nursed by his own Hebrew *mother*. Moses's *wife* Zipporah saved Moses from being killed by God. According to the early chapters of Exodus, God used a bunch of women to save the day. And yes, I never noticed this until a woman pointed it out. Have you recognized this? If you're a woman, maybe you have.

It's not just women, but all types of people. Hanging out with poor people has helped me see God's heart for the poor. Talking with a prostitute—no, I wasn't giving her business— helped me see God's passion for saving prostitutes. Studying the Bible with my African brothers and sisters has helped me see that several significant characters in the Bible were black, including Moses' second wife. My Asian friends, who grew up in an "honor-shame" culture, have helped me see that the Bible itself uses honor-shame categories when it retells the biblical story (for example, Genesis 2 and Hebrews 12).

If all I do is read Scripture through my white, middle-class, male lenses, and if I pursue God in a community with other white, middle-class men, I'm bound to miss out on the fullness of God, which is best revealed through a diverse community of image bearers. We're all prone to think about God through the homogeneous lenses we've grown up with. Fellowshipping with a diverse group of believers will help us see God and the world in high definition.[10] It's like that old joke where a guy asks a fish, "How's the water?" and the fish responds, "What's water?" It's easy to become so accustomed to what's around you that you forget that what's normal for you might seem strange to others.[11]

Fourth, diversity helps us love all types of people. On the flip side, homogeneity can prevent us from understanding and therefore loving people. If you only surround yourself with people like you, it's easy to grow less compassionate, less empathetic, and less loving toward "the other." Yet Christianity welcomes the stranger, the foreigner, the outside, the marginalized—the other. Since God loves all types of people, this should be one of the goals of discipleship if we're seeking to be like God.

I used to look down on homeless people. Every time I'd drive by one of those guys with a sign by the freeway exit asking for money, I'd just get annoyed, look away, and speed off, grumbling to myself, "Oh, go get a job!" I've never been homeless. Not even close. I have so many safety nets surrounding me that it would be really hard for me to end up on the streets. I would have to *want* to become homeless. And for many years, I projected my life circumstances onto every homeless person: They could go get a job if they weren't so darn lazy. They must *want* to be on the streets.

Maybe some do. But it wasn't until I started talking to and befriending homeless people that I realized that many don't. One guy I met has a master's degree in English. He used to have a home and a family and all the bells and whistles that come with a middle-class life. But one day as he was driving down a narrow country road, a truck backed out in front of him and he slammed into it going full speed. He was severely injured, which led to ongoing physical problems. Soon afterward, he lost his job, and then his wife, and then his house, and then his sobriety, and within a couple of years his middle-class rug was pulled out from under him, flopping him onto the streets of Springfield, Ohio. As he was telling me his story, slurping his soup through his thick homeless beard, I immediately thought: *That could be me. That could be anyone.*

Homelessness is terrible, but the diversity of homeless people is beautiful. I've gotten to know war veterans, construction workers, vagabonds, former bankers, mothers, fathers, and children. Each story is unique. Some have hope. Many don't. Some choose to be there, while many would love to get back on their feet but lack the psychological and spiritual strength to do so. They don't necessarily need food; they need a friend. And a Savior.

If I never took the time to hang out with homeless people, I'd still be zipping past the people holding signs with my self-righteous pedal to the metal. (Okay, sometimes I still do.) Getting to know people who live in a different socio-economic world than my own has not only expanded my view of God but also cultivated a love for God's beautiful and diverse people. It's helped me take one more step toward Christlikeness because he left his heavenly throne room to love people living in the gutter.

The same goes for ethnicity. Right after high school, I attended a college where I was the ethnic minority. It was Southwestern College in Chula Vista, California, just ten minutes north of the Mexico border. Most of the students were either Latino or Asian; a few were African American or Pacific Islander. Only a small percentage were white. I remember walking into my first class and instantly feeling out of place. Within seconds, I met eyes with the other two white people in class. A strange sense of camaraderie and familiarity warmed my body—I wasn't alone.

Besides feeling like an ethnic minority, I became friends with people from many different backgrounds. I could feel the ethnic roadblocks being pulled away as I journeyed toward the multiethnic heart of God. If God became human flesh to identify with and experience humanity, then in order to reflect the rhythm of God, we too should integrate ourselves into the lives of all God's image bearers.

Living in homogeneous communities stifles our love for other people. Ignorance of "the other" often breeds fear; fear prevents love; and lack of love prevents us from living like Jesus.

There are many other ways in which worshiping in diverse Christian communities helps us become more like Jesus. But before we close this chapter, I want to address a common question that comes up.

What If My Neighborhood Isn't Diverse?

This is usually the first question that comes up every time I talk about ethnic reconciliation. I've raised it several times myself! After all, I live in the fine state of Idaho, where 92 percent of the population is Caucasian. Most ethnic minorities in my state are clustered in particular neighborhoods. If churches reflect the diversity of their neighborhoods, then in Idaho they're probably not going to be very diverse. What do we do about this?

First, as a general principle, local churches should reflect the diversity of the neighborhoods where they are.[12] If a church is in neighborhood that's 90 percent Caucasian, then we should generally expect 10 percent of its members to be ethnic minorities. The problem is that most churches do not reflect the diversity of their surrounding communities. Also, many churches have a strong commuter population. In other words, most churches are not "neighborhood-only" churches, where people live within a mile of their church. Given the fact that churches aren't just made up of people from the neighborhood, we should expect much more diversity than actually exists, since we're not constrained by the ethnic makeup of the neighborhood.

A multiethnic gospel will attract a multiethnic group of people. The question is, are we preaching a gospel that shatters ethnic boundaries as Jesus and Paul did?

Second, even if a community isn't ethnically diverse, it's certainly going to be diverse in terms of gender, age, and maybe even socioeconomic status. Although neighborhoods often don't reflect socioeconomic diversity, they're usually more diverse than you think. It's not uncommon for one economically well-off community to be within five minutes of a lower-middle-class or impoverished neighborhood. If these two people groups are isolated from one another, God's kingdom vision is not being realized. If a church makes older people feel as if they aren't part of the family, then something's wrong. When the younger people miss out, everyone misses out.

The point is, there's probably much more diversity in your neighborhood than you realize. If you look for it, you'll be surprised at what you might find.

Third, work harder. The fact is, *most churches that are 90 percent Caucasian are located in communities much more diverse than that.* If—or because—this is the case, we need to ask some hard questions. *Why* are our churches not diverse? Are our members making disciples of all nations—the nations around them? If not, why? Is there anything about the church community that unknowingly makes minorities feel unwelcome or out of place because of their ethnic heritage? Are the cultural customs of the church (music, art, order of service) diverse or monolithic? Is everyone on stage white? Or black? What does this say about the values and perceived gifts of the church?

I could spend a whole separate chapter talking about the unforeseen ways in which the tone of our churches inevitably reflects its dominant culture, thereby marginalizing the minority. But here's what you can do: Ask a few different ethnic minorities in your church what they think. Have they felt like they have to *assimilate,* or do they feel like the church is genuinely *integrating* different cultures into its service and philosophy of ministry?

Fourth, get beyond the walls. Every church is part of the global church. Even if it's unrealistic to create a diverse community within a local church, partnering with a multiethnic or an ethnically different church would be a great step toward broadcasting the gospel that Jesus and Paul preached.

Did you know that a major focus of Paul's missionary journeys was to bring ethnic reconciliation to churches across the Mediterranean Sea? Throughout his journeys, Paul visited various Gentile-dominant churches in Greece and Asia Minor (Turkey) and asked them to give money to the impoverished Jewish Christians in Jerusalem. One of the goals, besides helping the poor, was to alleviate the ethnic tensions that divided the different churches—churches that existed hundreds of miles from one another. Paul says the Gentile-dominant churches "were glad to do this because they feel they owe a real debt to" the Jewish-Christian churches in Jerusalem. "Since the Gentiles received the spiritual blessings of the Good News from the believers in Jerusalem, they feel the least they can do in return is to help them financially" (Romans 15:27, NLT). In fact, Paul spends more ink writing about his adventure in ethnic reconciliation than he does writing about the doctrine of justification by faith.[13] In his eyes, the two go hand in hand.

What if we did stuff like this? What if we partnered with other ethnically diverse churches in the area? Even though my hometown of Boise appears to be as white as a leper on a winter day, I've recently found out that within a two-mile radius downtown, there's an African American Baptist church; an international church of African immigrants and refugees (the service is translated from English to Swahili);

three other churches made up of Eritrean, Nepalese, and Bhutanese refugees; and another church that meets with the homeless. All of these churches gather within a couple of miles of each other. What would happen if these churches somehow tried to work together, eat together, do ministry with one another, and serve one another? Well, it would be messy for sure! Reconciliation isn't easy. That's why we need Jesus at the center, as both our goal and our strength.

But it would be worth it. Because the gospel is worth it. Jesus is worth it. And all those involved would become a little more like Jesus as they became reconciled to other believers who worship the same Lord—who reconciled us all to himself.

A MORE SIMPLE WAY

I NEVER IN A MILLION YEARS wanted to plant a church. If you had asked me five years ago, or even five months ago, "Would you ever consider planting a church?" I would have laughed in your face. I've never had the desire, time, skills, or money to pull off a church plant. There are many church-planter types out there. And I'm definitely not one of them.

This is why my next phrase is comically ironic: *My family and I are in the process of planting a church.* I'd better give some backstory to this whole mess I've gotten myself into.

For several years, I've not felt that I fit in with the typical church culture. Remember my discussion about outliers back in chapter 5? Well, okay, so I'm an outlier. I don't really love church services. I'd rather listen to Coldplay than Chris Tomlin. I don't have time for superficial, Christianized conversations where everyone is "doing good" as they smile the pain away. I love to talk about God's Word—I'm a Bible professor at a Bible college—but I'd much rather have a discussion than give (or listen to) a monologue. I like to wrestle with hard theological questions, and I'm okay with not having all the right answers. I really enjoy hanging out with unbelievers, especially unbelievers who are poor. And I'd much rather be out in the community, tangibly showing the love of Jesus, than sitting in a pew listening to a sermon about the love of Jesus. Yes, I'll admit it. I am that guy.

I'm going to be brutally honest in this chapter. This may be the most raw and real chapter of the book—perhaps of any book I've written. Some of the things I say in this chapter might frustrate you. Other things might bring a sigh of relief from your lungs. I want to ask for a bit of grace from you if I overstate things or misrepresent the state of the church. I don't mean to be critical or cynical. I truly do love the bride of Christ and I believe the church is doing some amazing things to reach people for Christ.

But I do want to be honest with where I'm at in my journey—a journey that has led me kicking and screaming into the church-planting business. It all started several years ago when I began to question the church's use of money.

Do We Really Need That Chandelier?

For years, I've been troubled by how many churches spend money—*God's* money, as we call it. When I'm in church,

I often look around at all the sound equipment, chandeliers, carpets, decorations, and everything else that's "necessary" to pull off a church service week after week. I'm not a trouble-maker, so I usually keep my mouth shut. But I've often wondered: Is all this stuff necessary for discipleship? Are there other ways that we could spend our money that would more effectively further the kingdom of God? If we pulled way back on our church expenses, would we be able to send more missionaries overseas? Or rescue little girls from sex trafficking? Or help the poor around us?

Speaking of missionaries, I often think of the ones who are undersupported, or have returned home because their support ran dry. I think of the many aspiring missionaries who never got off the ground because they couldn't raise enough funds. I think of the two billion people in the world who live on less than two dollars a day—millions of whom are Christians, our very own brothers and sisters. Or the one billion people who don't have adequate access to clean water. Or the 1.5 billion people who live without electricity. I think of other needs at home, in our own communities. The home-less, the widows, the elderly, the ten thousand refugees who live in my hometown of Boise. By the time you finish this chapter, more than three hundred children will have died because of hunger or malnutrition.[1]

I look at all of this and I can no longer look away. American Christians give 50 to 60 billion dollars to the church every year. About 18 percent of this money goes toward the cost of church buildings. The real estate owned by churches in America is worth over $230 billion.[2] According to Richard Stearns, president of World Vision:

> Simply stated, [the American Church] is the
> wealthiest community of Christians in the history
> of Christendom. How wealthy? The total income of
> American churchgoers is $5.2 trillion. . . . It would
> take just a little over 1 percent of the income of
> American Christians to lift the poorest one billion
> people in the world out of extreme poverty.[3]

Have we made Christianity in America too expensive? Are we spending God's money on the things that he would spend it on? Are all the resources (time, energy, personnel, and money) that go into pulling off church services every Sunday producing radical, Christlike disciples? (As we've seen in chapter 1, the answer is "no.") It just seems as if we've created an expensive machine called "church" that's so dependent upon money (and lots of it) that it's hard to sustain or reproduce. And the return—making disciples who make disciples—has been far less than what we should expect.

A friend of mine who used to be a megachurch pastor asked ten of his pastor friends these questions:

- If money weren't an issue, would you continue doing ministry the way you're doing it now?
- If you had unlimited funds, would you have the same programs, the same types of services, the same staff positions, and everything else that your church is devoted to?
- Would Sunday morning look the same?

You know what they said? Ten out of ten said, "No." Ten out of ten pastors admitted that at least some—or most—of what they've created is necessary because it keeps people happy and maintains a steady or growing attendance. A church that retains its people can pay the bills because more people means more tithe money. And more money helps sustain the expensive ministries we've created. And around and around we go.

PRIORITY CHURCH ASSIGNS TO DISCIPLESHIP

	All Church Leaders	Senior Pastors	Discipleship Leaders
Q: What priority does your church place on discipleship, relative to other ministries? Is it . . . ?			
Among the top 3 priorities	61%	62%	58%
The number one priority	26	26	28
Important, not one of the top 3 priorities	8	8	11
Not something you are actively addressing at this time	4	4	4
Not sure	1	1	0

PERCENT OF BUDGET SPENT ON DISCIPLESHIP

	All Church Leaders	Senior Pastors	Discipleship Leaders
Q: About what percent of your church's operational budget is spent on programs or resources specifically aimed at discipleship?			
Less than 10 percent	27%	26%	29%
10 to 19 percent	29	30	27
20 to 29 percent	18	20	15
30 percent or more	26	24	28
Mean	21	21	22
Median	15	15	15

On the flip side, if the pastor rocks the boat too much, implements ministries that turn people off, or cancels ministries that aren't helping people become more like Jesus, then people might leave. And if too many people leave, the church can't make budget to sustain all the ministries. Or it won't be able to pay its staff. Or, worst-case scenario, if enough people leave, then the pastor won't get paid.

Please don't get me wrong. I believe that most pastors are filled with integrity and aren't trying to make a lot of money from doing ministry. I believe most pastors truly desire more than anything to see people come to faith in Christ and then grow closer to Jesus through fellowship, teaching, Communion, and prayer (Acts 2:42). My concern isn't so much with the intention or motivation of church leaders. It's with the system of doing church that's been passed down to us (in America)—a system that's inherently expensive and often overly complicated.

In their book *Church Refugees,* Josh Packard and Ashleigh Hope interviewed one pastor to see how much time and energy was spent on each Sunday's ninety-minute service. Between prepping for the sermon, producing the podcast, setting up, tearing down, worship practice, and everything else that was necessary for the service, the pastor found that 137 hours a week and 60 percent of the church budget went into the weekly church service. The pastor himself was stunned. He didn't realize that so much of the church's time and money went into the Sunday service. And this particular church had only about a hundred members.[4] Imagine how much time and energy goes into the Sunday services for a church of a thousand or ten thousand.

I don't think there's anything inherently wrong with Sunday services. Christian gatherings are awesome and biblical. Much good can come from them. My main concern is with the way we've gone about Sunday services. They've largely become a resource hog and a spectator sport. People come, watch, listen, and leave. Clearly, the Bible commends the gathering of believers for fellowship, teaching, Communion, and prayer (Acts 2:42; Hebrews 10:24-25). But the way we've gone about these gatherings has become cluttered with many complex and expensive add-ons that aren't mandated, nor envisioned, by the Bible. Nor are they necessary for—or even effective at—helping people become more like Christ.

The statistics are clear: Our current systems of doing church are generally not producing disciples who make disciples.

The statistics are clear: Our current systems of doing church are generally not producing disciples who make disciples.[5] Virtually every church is faithful at Sunday services—and putting much time, energy, and money into them. But statistically, most churches are not doing a great job at making disciples who make disciples. Whatever we think about our way of doing church, something's missing.

I wonder whether there's a better way. A way in which most of the church's time, energy, personnel, and money could be spent on things that more effectively produce radical Jesus followers.

Simple Discipleship

The New Testament paints a strikingly simple portrait of disciple making. Jesus called people to follow him. Some people responded to the call and followed him. After his death, resurrection, and ascension, these people formed communities where they devoted themselves to fellowship, teaching, breaking bread, and prayer. And these communities embodied Jesus' call to discipleship by calling others to follow Jesus and join their community. As the church grew, it reproduced into small gatherings where believers continued to make disciples who made disciples.

It was simple. No bells and whistles. Just small gatherings of radical Jesus followers scattered throughout the Mediterranean world, testifying to the lordship of King Jesus over all things.

The first Christians still "tithed" part of their income to church.[6] Yet none of these tithes went to fund the machine we now call church. Since they met in homes or out in public (Acts 2:46), none of the money went to fund a building. There's no evidence that the money went to fund church programs or staff workers. Early church gatherings were shockingly inexpensive and simple.

There are two passages in the New Testament where Paul talks about some elders getting paid for their work (1 Corinthians 9:8-14; 1 Timothy 5:17-18). At the same time, Paul often chose *not* to take money when it would have hindered his ministry. Paul made money as a tentmaker to set an example for others, so that he wouldn't be a burden on the church (1 Corinthians 9:12). We also see evidence that some money went to fund missionaries and itinerant leaders (Romans 16:1-2). In fact, Jesus himself was supported by several wealthy women during his three-year ministry on earth (Luke 8:1-3). It's not wrong for pastors to get paid. But it's also not always necessary. Pastoring is not inherently linked to a paycheck.

Aside from funding some pastors and missionaries, the rest of the church's money went to help people in need, even if they lived hundreds of miles away (see Romans 15:25-29; 2 Corinthians 8–9; Galatians 2:10; and other passages).[7] What we see in the New Testament is radical generosity toward *people*. There was no such thing as an expensive church machine that sucked up most of the tithe money to keep the Sunday services going.

We shouldn't glorify the first-century church, of course. It certainly had its own problems (see Acts 6:1-6; Galatians 2:11-14; Philippians 4:2-3). But what we do see is an extremely simple way of doing church that was very effective at making disciples. One of my favorite scenes in the book of Acts comes at the beginning of chapter 17. Paul and Silas were preaching the gospel in the synagogues of Thessalonica, and they got kicked out. Before they left, a bunch of Gentiles at the synagogue believed Paul's message and became Christians. The Jews became jealous, so they formed a mob against the house of Jason, where Paul and Silas were staying. When they couldn't find Paul and Silas, they dragged out Jason and other Christians and accused them before the authorities. This is what they said: "These men who have *turned the world upside down* have come here also" (Acts 17:6, emphasis added).

Turned the world upside down. I love that phrase! Even though this little religion was but a speck on the map of the Roman world, they made such a dent in society that they were seen as turning the world upside down. And they did it at cost. No bells, no whistles. No programs or events. No stages or lights or expensive sound equipment. No paid staff, no buildings, no podcasts or radio shows.

None of these things are bad. There's nothing intrinsically wrong with sound equipment or stages. But when viewed against the backdrop of the massive decline of discipleship in the church today, we have to ask, *Is all this stuff worth it?*

Are we doing church the way we're doing it because we wholeheartedly believe that it's the most biblical and effective way to make disciples? (Few pastors I know say yes.) Or are we doing it because it's all we've ever known? And because people will get mad and leave if we try to introduce more simple and effective ways of helping people become more like Christ?

Playing into people's consumeristic felt needs is not the way of Christ. It's cowardice.

Playing into people's consumeristic felt needs is not the way of Christ. It's cowardice.

We Are Church

I long for a simpler version of church, where Jesus' disciples gather together for rich fellowship, an in-depth study of the apostle's teaching, a shared cup of wine and loaf of bread in remembrance of Christ's death, and intimate prayers. This is part of the reason why I've decided to plant a church. A simple church. A non-churchy church. A church where all the clutter is swept aside so that we can break bread together before we go out and share the love of Christ in our community.

At the time of writing, my family and I just got back from

San Francisco, where we met with a network of churches called We Are Church that grew out of the video series *Basic* by Francis Chan. Those videos lay the groundwork for a more simple and reproducible way of doing church. What started as one small church in 2012 has now grown into a network of eight different home-based fellowships scattered throughout San Francisco. And it looks as if my family and I are going to start a We Are Church fellowship here in Boise. But it's going to look quite different from most churches.

First of all, none of the pastors at We Are Church are paid. In fact, "doing church" costs exactly nothing. Nada. Nil. No money. One hundred percent of the tithes and offerings go toward the needs of the body of Christ (or outside the body) and furthering the mission of Christ. There's not a single ministry decision that's based on money. There's no pressure to grow in order to support staff salaries and building mortgages. As long as we're being faithful at becoming more like Christ and sharing his truth and love in the community, then it's really up to God to bring people in. And there's no pressure on my end if he delays.

Growth isn't bad. But let's face it. Most church growth is *transfer* growth, not *conversion* growth. Most churches grow because they're doing church in a way that's more appealing than the surrounding churches (better music, better programs, and more engaging preaching). And so Christians will leave one church for another church until another church pops up and puts on a better church service.

When a church has no financial burden, there's no pressure to create an attractive environment that will draw (mostly Christian) people to the church. Again, paying a pastor isn't wrong. It might be biblical. But not paying a pastor isn't wrong either. It might enable the church to reproduce itself more effectively.

Since We Are Church churches gather in homes, they are small. The smallness helps enable (though does not guarantee) a more relational, "family-like" gathering. No one sits on the sidelines or gets lost in the pews. Everyone is treated like a brother or sister or mother or father. And as we saw in chapter 3, genuine discipleship can't happen without relationships.

Now, as I'm sure you know, family can be messy! So let's not candy-coat the whole family metaphor. Gathering as a family doesn't mean that everyone will get along perfectly and that there won't be any relational problems. Quite the opposite! But what it does mean is that everyone will be committed to each other in love and truth.

After all, "love one another" is one of the most basic, fundamental Christian commands given to the church.

- "A new commandment I give to you, that you love one another: just as I have loved you, you also are to love one another" (John 13:34).
- "By this all people will know that you are my disciples, if you have love for one another" (John 13:35).
- "For this is the message that you have heard from the beginning, that we should love one another" (1 John 3:11).
- "And this is his commandment, that we believe in the name of his Son Jesus Christ and love one another, just as he has commanded us" (1 John 3:23).

- "Greater love has no one than this, that someone lay down his life for his friends" (John 15:13).
- "You shall love your neighbor as yourself" (which Jesus says is the second greatest command, next to "Love the Lord your God"—Matthew 22:37-39).

Most people come to church, chitchat for a few minutes, and then attend a service where 95 percent or more of the people sit and watch other people using their gifts. Then when the service is over, parents rush off to get their kids from Sunday school, and if there's a second service about to start, they need to do this rather quickly. Some people may connect with other people on a deep, intimate level. But in my twenty years of "doing church" at twelve different churches, belonging to four different denominations in three different states and three different countries, I can confidently say that for the majority of churchgoers, Sunday morning is not the time to love or be loved.

It's also not usually the time to ask hard questions. Or serve the poor. Or share Jesus with unbelievers. Or help other believers in need. Or do a whole bunch of other things that Christians are to do. Again, church services aren't bad. They can be a wonderful time of worship and teaching. But it does appear that by itself, attending church services—even really good ones—is not producing the types of disciples Jesus intends to create.

At We Are Church, even though the pastors aren't paid, they are still training up other pastors and multiplying churches. Even though forty-five-minute sermons aren't preached every Sunday, everyone in the church is reading through the Bible and discussing it on Sundays and throughout the week with each other. Even though there aren't any programs, the lost are being reached, the youth are being discipled, and communities are being touched by the love of these radical Jesus followers. Even though there's no worship band or expensive sound equipment, every week believers cry out to Jesus through songs of praise.

Francis Chan told me a beautiful story about a time when one of the house churches gathered together for worship, but the worship leader—a girl with a guitar and a good voice—couldn't make it to the gathering. At first, no one knew what to do. How can we worship God without a skilled musician? So one of the members, an ex-con who recently got saved, stepped forward and started belting out songs of praise to Jesus. He had a terrible voice: totally off-key. No band, no guitar, no stage, no sound system. Yet everyone joined in with authentic, heart-pounding worship. And tears flooded the room.

When I hear stories like this, I just wonder whether we have overly professionalized the church's worship of its holy Creator. What would happen if we explored simpler, more dimmed-down, more authentic ways to worship Jesus—the one who said "the true worshipers will worship the Father in spirit and truth" (John 4:23)?

Smaller home-based gatherings like this are not perfect. They're messy and difficult and come with their own set of trials. My point is to give a tangible example of church that is done more simply, cost-efficiently, and authentically. And this more stripped-down version of church is still doing all the things that God calls the church to do.

The Church in Nepal Is Killing It—Simply

Along with being a college professor, writer, and (now) church planter (sort of), I'm also part of a ministry called Touch Nepal. Every year, some friends and I go over to Nepal to hang out with the ministry leaders we support. It's always an eye-opening experience. I'll never forget my first visit. One of the Nepalese pastors took us out to the middle of a jungle, where we were supposed to attend a church service. We must have been driving out in the middle of nowhere for two hours before I wondered, *Did we take a wrong turn? Should I tell our driver that he must be on the wrong road?* There was no civilization for miles around.

But then the jungle opened up and we found ourselves in the midst of a village that looked like it was straight out of the eighteenth century: donkeys, carriages, wooden carts, thatched roofs, smolder fires. I was waiting for Bilbo to pop out of his hobbit hole. The van stopped—apparently, we were at the right spot for the church service—but I didn't see any church building or people wearing suits and ties.

Then I heard it. Coming from a broken-down, barn-like building thundered the sound of forty Nepalese believers worshiping Jesus in a room that should have held twenty-five people at best.

A couple of people ushered us to the front of the room as the believers kept belting out songs of praise to Jesus. We walked to the front, turned around, sat down facing the congregation, and met many smiling faces as they continued to cry out to their God.

This church was truly amazing. And it was simple. The

pastor received a small stipend for his work but held a second job to provide income. The building was nothing more than an old barn with a room upstairs. No one else was paid. It costs hardly anything to come together and worship. Unlikely converts were being made. Most of them were saved out of Hinduism; they were ostracized by their families and, in some cases, brutally persecuted. Yet they kept singing at the top of their lungs. They kept preaching to their neighbors about a risen Savior who now rules the earth and its jungles.

A simple church with hardly any funds, no real building, a part-time pastor, no programs, and no stage. And they turned the world upside down because they were empowered by the Holy Spirit of God.

While Christianity is declining in America, it is growing like crazy in the impoverished little country of Nepal. Fifteen years ago, Christians made up only 0.5 percent of the country. Now, over 2.5 percent are committed Christ followers. Much of this growth has come without all the expensive church stuff that we have here in America. Along with that lost-in-the-jungle church, I've visited several other gatherings in Nepal, and all of them are incredibly simple. There's fellowship. Teaching. Food. Prayer. More food. And piles and piles of love spilling over from one believer to another. When I read in Acts 4 about early Christians gathering as "one heart and soul, and no one said that any of the things that belonged to him was his own, but they had everything in common" (Acts 4:32), it makes me think of the church in Nepal—the church that's growing five times faster than the church in America.

I know things are different in the United States. We're not a majority-world country. We have money to spend on buildings and salaries and all the additions we've made to our church gatherings. But just because we have it doesn't mean we have to spend it. I truly believe that if we can implement a more simple way of doing church, we might just see more disciples being made—and made more effectively.

Moving toward a Simpler Church

No model of church is perfect. Every model has its pros and cons. I'm not arguing for a particular model of doing church. I'm arguing for a more simple way of doing church, no matter the model.

I'm arguing that worship leaders should explore more simple and cost-efficient ways to lead people in worship. Powerfully lifting our voices in communal praise should not cost so much, nor should it take hours to rehearse.

I'm suggesting that church leaders should reevaluate their budgets to see if what they're spending money on truly reflects the values of Christ. If Jesus were in charge of your budget, would it look the same? If not, then it needs to change.

I'm urging lay Christians to view themselves not as mere "lay Christians" but as Spirit-endowed followers of the King who have gifts that can turn the world upside down.

I'm asking pastors to consider implementing the most *faithful* type of ministry—even if it means taking a financial hit—because any ministry that's dictated by money is a disobedient ministry.

I'm challenging local churches to ask a hard question:

What can we cut out of our church machine to make room for more effective ways of creating disciples who make disciples?

I'm urging all Christians to put into practice the central command to "love one another." If your church experience does not include loving each other authentically, then you're not experiencing church the way God intended.

Growing Disciples by Leaps and Bounds!

In early church times, "the disciples were increasing in numbers by leaps and bounds" (Acts 6:1, MSG). We in the Navigator Church Ministries come alongside pastors, leaders, and kingdom laborers to help make this a reality—to grow cultures where disciple making is happening wherever people live, work, and play. We partner with churches to see God's Word come alive in hearts and lives as values shift from information to transformation, from programs to process. We are accomplishing more for the advance of the gospel by doing less. Commitment to modeling, maturity, and multiplication of life-to-life disciple making is caught and taught. Churches then experience the joy in sending out disciples who truly do make disciples!

ROY AND MARGARET FITZWATER,
codirectors of Navigator Church Ministries

Personally, I've found that the house church can be a great vehicle for carrying these things out. It's simple and efficient, and if it has solid leadership, it can reproduce itself more easily and effectively. But it's not the only model. I know several effective churches that maintain a traditional way of doing church, and yet have gotten rid of all the add-ons that aren't helping Christians follow Christ more faithfully. They're stripped down, financially efficient (and generous), authentic, and making a massive dent in their communities with the love of Christ.[8]

Whatever the model, don't let the cultural clutter get in the way of making disciples of all nations.

Also, let's not overcomplicate the call of Christ. Jesus said, "Follow me, and I will make you fishers of men" (Matthew 4:19) and "Go therefore and make disciples of all nations" (Matthew 28:19-20). Shortly after that, the Spirit fell upon these believers, and they went out and started to make disciples.

So let's do that. Let's make this basic Christian command more central to the values of church.

Some of Jesus' disciples were literate; most were illiterate. None of them were pastors with seminary degrees. Yet they turned the world upside down by making disciples. Maybe it's our overly professionalized culture, I don't know. But the fact is that many Christians feel that they don't have all the right tools or all the biblical answers to disciple people. Of course, I'm all for becoming more biblically literate and making sure you're seeking Christ before you tell others to. But let's not overly complicate the command. Jesus says, "Follow me; then go make disciples and help them follow Christ." He doesn't say, "Make sure you've got all the answers before you make fishers of men." He doesn't tell only Bible study leaders or Sunday school teachers or paid pastors who have it all together to make disciples. It's a command to all Christians.

So let's go. Let's do this. Let's do what Jesus tells us to do.

LET'S GO!

As I THINK BACK through all the stuff we've talked about in this book, it's hard not to be discouraged about all the things we need to do to become more like Christ. And as I look into my own life, there are several ideas I've articulated in this book that I'm not implementing in my life as much as I should.

If you're feeling this way too, then be encouraged. This book isn't about setting unattainable standards or even trying to master the full gamut of the Christian life overnight. It's about reevaluating what it means to become like Christ in light of the Bible and asking God to show us the way. It's about being self-critical, reformational, always eager to reexamine our perceived notions of what it means to follow Christ in light of Scripture to see if we're doing it rightly.

The post-Reformers used to say, *Ecclesia semper reformanda est*, or "The church is [reformed and] always reforming." The Reformers regularly returned to Scripture and celebrated its ultimate authority over all belief and practice. They were not just *reformed* (that is, Protestant) but also *reforming*—constantly—in light of Scripture. This should be an ongoing posture, not a one-time event. The church should regularly drag traditionally held ideas and practices back to the Bible and eagerly demand reexamination.

It's common for unexamined beliefs to become detached from their scriptural roots through time and repetition. We assume that the way we've always done it should be the way we always do it. But if we believe the Bible is our final and ultimate authority over everything we think and do, then the Bible—not tradition—must be our guide.

This book is an attempt to do just that. To reexamine what it means to be a disciple of Christ, to "become more like Jesus."

Now let me let you in on a little secret when it comes to writing a book. One of the main questions any writer must ask is *Who's your audience? To whom are you writing?* Whom do you envision reading this book as you're writing it? To be honest, I've had three different audiences in view: pastors, lay leaders, and general Christians who take their faith seriously. And when it comes to implementing the ideas of this book—assuming you think that at least some of what I've said is worth implementing!—this will probably look different for pastors, lay leaders, and general Christians. (I actually don't love the term "general Christian," by the way, but hopefully you get the point and aren't offended.)

So let me close with a down-to-earth conversation about how all of us can apply what we've talked about.

Pastors

I imagine that if you pastor a large church in a diverse neighborhood with well-polished Sunday services and plentiful programs and members who are mostly wealthy and white— well, you may be angry or depressed.

If you're angry, my only question is, do you find the stuff I've talked about in the book unbiblical? And if so, why? Where? What chapter and verse? Make sure your anger is justified. Disagreement isn't refutation. It's just a reaction.

If you're depressed, it's probably because you agree with much of what I've said, and yet you don't know where to start. Here's my advice to you: Don't try to change things overnight. If you see several areas in your philosophy of ministry that need to change, take them one at a time. Even if it takes ten or twenty or thirty years to become a more faithful, Jesus-like, disciple-making church, that's okay. Rome wasn't built in a day, and neither was the kingdom of God. It's still under construction.

After all, this is how we should pursue Christ on an individual level. There's no way we can carry out all the demands of Christ all the time starting tomorrow. We can't physically witness to the lost; help the poor; visit people in prison; care for the orphan, the widow, the elderly, the homeless, and the refugee; disciple our kids; love our spouses; study the Bible; pray without ceasing; care for our relatives; mentor younger believers; help with setting up and tearing down at church on Sundays; and still have time to watch Netflix. Even if we cancel Netflix, we still can't do it all. Not all at once, at least. We need to cultivate a rhythm of life that reflects Christ. The same is true of ministry.

Don't try to change things overnight. This will probably destroy the church. Instead, introduce things slowly. Perhaps introduce a "year of simplicity" where you have a more simple style of worship (one person with a guitar) and no bells and whistles during the service (whatever they may be: lights, graphics, or background slides on the screen during worship, which are pretty distracting anyway). Maybe you could have a goal of giving away twice as much money to missions as you have in previous years. The key is to get people on board—get them excited about living and worshiping more simply so that they can see Christ more clearly.

One of the churches in Southern California, where I was a teaching elder, used to hold a "Celebrate Generosity" Sunday every year on its anniversary. All of the tithes and offerings that came into the church that week went to fund outside ministries we were involved in. Fifty percent went to help other local church plants we were connected with, and the other 50 percent went to overseas missions work we were involved in (including Touch Nepal). It's crazy, but Celebrate Generosity is always the largest giving Sunday of the year. People love to give to tangible needs, especially needs where there's some sort of relational connection. Last year, the church gave more than $100,000 on Celebrate Generosity. And the church only has a few hundred members.

If you desire to raise the intellectual bar in your church (chapter 6), then maybe you could orchestrate your own City Forums, or a Sunday night gathering focused on engaging in relevant topics and modeling critical thinking and dialogue. Maybe read through an intellectually rigorous book with your leaders to get them on board. (I'd highly recommend Mark Noll's *The Scandal of the Evangelical Mind*.) Or preach a sermon series on loving God with our minds. The key is to show people that good thinking is part of good discipleship. Chances are that your people are probably hungering for more depth anyway.

If you believe your church is too segregated (chapter 8) and doesn't reflect the multicultural heart of God, you can begin by having people of different ethnic backgrounds preach at your church or lead worship. You could reach out and befriend other ethnically different congregations in your city. Get to know their leaders and members, and see how you could partner together. If you are hiring for a position, try to hire someone of a different ethnic background than other leaders at your church (assuming they're qualified for the position, of course). Get to know the ethnic minorities who *are* in your church. Ask *them* whether they feel like they have to assimilate to fit in or whether their ethnic heritage is honored and integrated in your church.

Since the Bible is filled with stories of scandalous grace (chapter 2), a good place to start is by preaching on grace. Read Jonathan Dodson's *Gospel-Centered Discipleship* or Philip Yancey's *What's So Amazing about Grace?* or—at the risk of self-promotion—my own book *Charis: God's Scandalous Grace for Us*. Then preach and teach about this radical grace. If people aren't offended, you're probably not preaching grace as faithfully as you ought to. The grace that Jesus preached offended the religious.

Creating a more missional church (chapter 7) is rather easy, since most people are so hungry for it. I've seen many churches ignite a fire in their people when it starts engaging the community in tangible ways. There will be some people, of course, who will accuse you of teaching a "social gospel." But don't let this scare you. Sure, implementing Christless, gospel-less outreach doesn't reflect the heart of Jesus. But neither does ignoring the social aspects of the gospel out of fear that stubborn Christians will cut off their tithe money or leave the church if you start talking about the poor. If you believe it's biblical—and it is—then you should make sure your people are engaging in the mission of Christ, if indeed you want them to become more like Christ.

Again, my main advice is to take it slow. Focus on one or two areas where your church needs to change in order to be more effective at making disciples.

Lay Leaders

A lay leader is someone who has some sort of leadership role at his or her church, even if he or she doesn't get paid for it. To be clear, the Bible itself doesn't make the distinction between lay leaders and paid leaders as two different vocations. The Bible only talks about elders and deacons. Some of the teaching elders might get paid, but this doesn't mean they occupy some higher office. The qualifications for paid and unpaid elders are the same.

Being a lay leader can be awesome. You get to help out in the church, but you usually don't bear the administrative or pastoral burden of the church. Lay leaders tend to sleep better at night, especially Saturday nights. But being a lay leader can also be frustrating. Sometimes we feel like second-class leaders, since we're not in on all the conversations and meetings that the paid staff are in at the church. Or sometimes our gifts and leadership abilities are less valued because we're not getting paid. I'll never forget when a seminary-trained paid pastor told my friend who was a lay elder, "You're one of the best *lay* teachers I've ever heard." The paid pastor was actually a terrible teacher: excessively dull, unclear, and irrelevant. He couldn't teach his way out of a wet paper bag. My friend— the mere *lay* teacher—was ten times better than the pastor. He just didn't take a paycheck for it.

So what can we do with this weird space we find ourselves in? It all depends on the relationship you have with the other leaders of the church. In one sense, I'd recommend that you seek to implement things in the same way that the pastor should (see the previous section). But you'll have a harder time doing this if the other leaders aren't on board. (Paid pastors generally have much more pull in introducing changes than lay leaders do.) In any case, here are some general recommendations.

First, go about it in a humble way. If you see changes that should be made—maybe some programs that aren't contributing to people's growth in Christlikeness—don't storm the next elder meeting and call everyone on the carpet. Whatever insight you may have is best introduced in a humble way, not claiming to have all the right answers but wishing instead to reexamine some things in light of Scripture. And as I said above, don't try to suggest too many changes at once. Maybe focus on one and humbly talk to the leaders about it.

Second, talk about your concerns on a relational level with

other leaders. Talk to your pastor or your fellow elders. Don't rally the troops in your Bible study and cause them to think badly of the church or its leaders. That's called gossip and spreading discord—and God hates this (Proverbs 6:29). Be sensitive to where people are, not frustrated because they're not where you think they should be.

Third, by all means, don't go all Nehemiah on people in public. (Read Nehemiah 13:25. It's really funny and scary at the same time.) Don't publicly call out the people in your Bible study for being segregated. If you're up on stage, don't condemn the stage, the lights, the sound equipment, and the worship leader for buying the new projector when he should have sent the money to Nepal. If you go against the leadership and try to change the church by yourself, you'll probably end up splitting the church—and then no one wins.

Fourth, start doing it in your own life. Find time to get to know the needs in your community. Visit another ethnically diverse church in town and get to know its pastor. Figure out ways in which you can live more simply and give more money away to people in need. Read some books on grace and ask the Lord to show where you are still trying to earn his favor through performance. Dive into your church community more wholeheartedly and *demonstrate* community. Get to know some of the Millennials at your church and listen to their questions, passions, and doubts.

General Christians

Okay, so I guess if you're not a pastor or a leader, you're just a general Christian. A plain old average pew sitter. I'm kidding, of course. Actually—whether you believe this or not—you have the same Spirit of God dwelling in you, and your gifts are just as vital, just as valuable, and just as powerful as the gifts that the Spirit has given to your leaders. The kingdom of God has been advancing on the backs of "general" Christians for the last two thousand years.

Most Christians who don't have some sort of formal leadership role at church have a hard time implementing changes in the way we do church. The way things are usually set up, ministry decisions flow from the top down. This isn't necessarily bad (depending on the leadership). It's just the way things are. Start living this stuff out in your own life before you try to get the church on board.

If you're really passionate about creating a better discipleship climate at church, you could propose a new ministry to the leadership that would help people become more like Jesus. Maybe it's a new outreach to the poor in the community (like that laundry ministry I talked about in chapter 7).

If you want to create a more traditional church ministry, make sure it's authentic and effective at helping people become more like Christ. Maybe lead people through a Christian book that will shake them up a bit rather than affirm the status quo. If you're more of an outlier, share your heart with the leaders and help them see how your outside-the-box ministry can further God's kingdom among fellow outliers of society. Tell your leaders about the various unbelievers you're reaching out to, and invite them into your ministry to them.

Now here's the thing. There's a chance—maybe a good chance, depending on your church—that your idea will get shot down. This is one of the biggest complaints among people who leave the church. They say that all their ideas were shot down by the professional ministers who apparently had all the right ministries already in place. I know this can be discouraging, but if this happens to you, try not to get discouraged. Try again. Think of another ministry. If all your ideas keep getting shot down, then have an honest conversation with the leaders and share your heart. And—pay attention to this—be open to the possibility that your ideas are not actually good ideas. Don't be so prideful that you simply assume you are right and your leaders are wrong. If they are truly called by God to lead the church, then there's a good chance that they may see things in your ideas that aren't biblical or don't fit within the ministry philosophy of the church.

That said, there's a chance you are right and they are wrong. Ministry philosophies aren't inspired by God, and they can sometimes hinder creative kingdom-advancement ventures from blossoming. Seek counsel from a diverse group of godly people. Have them examine your idea. Search the Scriptures, pray hard, and talk to your leaders again. If you are constantly stonewalled from using your gifts in ministry at your church, then it may be time to find another church.

I don't say this lightly. I almost didn't want to say it at all! I'm not an advocate of hopping around from church to church, or leaving a church anytime you disagree with its leaders. This isn't what I'm saying. If you must leave a church, do so humbly, graciously, and openly, seeking forgiveness from anyone you've sinned against.

Go

God's kingdom transcends any one church. It's expansive and dynamic; it can't be contained within the walls of any one church. It covers your community and is expanding into the county. It's manifested in every place where believers are gathered and advancing good through the gospel. This kingdom cannot be shaken, and it cannot be stopped. You can kill it, stab it, and crucify it, but it will never die. It will only multiply. God's reign over the nations will prevail, and the gates of hell don't stand a chance.

So we must go. We cannot stay put. We cannot pursue the American dream, for this land is not our land—we belong to another kingdom. God's kingdom. The global reign of God through his image bearers. And God has released his Spirit in you so that you can incarnate the love of Christ to a dying world.

So go. Go do that. Go make disciples of all the nations. And I'll see you on the other side.

Afterword

We've heard it a hundred times, but I wonder how deeply Jesus' words actually penetrate our hearts?

> All authority in heaven and on earth has been given to me. Go therefore and make disciples of all nations, baptizing them in the name of the Father and of the Son and of the Holy Spirit, teaching them to observe all that I have commanded you.
>
> MATTHEW 28:18-20

Once we, as Christ followers, have tasted and seen that the Lord is good, once we have experienced the grace of God as revealed in Christ, once we have been given new life through the death and resurrection of Jesus—we're to go. Go and make disciples. It's that simple. And it's not just a calling for missionaries and pastors; it's for every person, in the context of everyday life.

When The Navigators joined forces with the Barna Group to take the pulse of discipleship in America, we weren't overly surprised at the findings. Lots of anecdotal evidence exists to suggest that, very often, what we've been doing in the American church has not been resulting in robust, mature disciples of Jesus. In fact, the research reveals story after story of people whose exposure to Christianity has left them unengaged in the things of God. The Barna research gave concrete evidence of what we had all come to suspect, even to assume. There's more work to be done in building strong foundations in the lives of those who say "yes" to Jesus.

We were relieved to also learn from Barna's research that our work—the work of The Navigators—was resulting in what we might call "discipleship outliers." People who had been discipled through The Navigators were seen to take more joy in the life of discipleship, to show more command of and interest in the Scriptures, and to be more invested in Jesus' great commission to not just settle only in their own spirituality, but to actually go and make disciples right where they are—where they live, work, study, and play.

There's nothing all that magical about the ministry of The Navigators. It boils down to basics—what I refer to in another work as "traits of a Christ follower":

- Walking with Jesus
- Knowing and living the Scriptures

- Participating in community
- Engaging with those who don't know Christ
- Reproducing spiritual generations[1]

There are all kinds of other good things associated with the Christian life. But as Preston demonstrates in this book, sometimes good things take the place of the first things. And when that happens, we slowly drift away from that simple, straightforward purpose we hear from the lips of Jesus: Be disciples *and* go and make disciples. Know Christ and make him known.

That, I think, is the main message to take away from *Go: Returning Discipleship to the Front Lines of Faith.* We don't have to give up the many good things that God puts before us. We just can't lose sight of the first things. It's those first things that move us along in our God-given purpose, whether we're homemakers, executives, teachers, construction workers, or computer scientists. It's those first things that bless the people we love and care about in the most fundamental, most eternal ways. And it's those first things that fortify our own faith as we invest ourselves in the eternity of others around us. It's those first things that fill our discipleship with joy.

Doug Nuenke
US President of The
Navigators

Notes

CHAPTER 1—A HOMELESS PEASANT BORN IN A FEEDING TROUGH: THE SCANDAL OF FOLLOWING JESUS

1. Dietrich Bonhoeffer, *The Cost of Discipleship* (New York: Touchstone, 1959), 77.
2. *The State of Discipleship: A Barna Report Produced in Partnership with The Navigators* (2015).
3. Christian Smith and Melinda Lundquist Denton, *Soul Searching: The Religious and Spiritual Lives of American Teenagers,* 2nd ed. (Oxford: Oxford University Press, 2009).
4. Smith and Denton, *Soul Searching,* 164.
5. Interestingly, the rest of the New Testament—Romans through Revelation—doesn't use the term *disciple.* Some people have tried to make a big stink out of this. But the absence of the word *disciple* outside of the Gospels and Acts doesn't seem to be a big deal. Other, similar terms are used after Acts, such as "believers," "holy ones," "children of God," and other intimate terms like "brother and sister." These are used to describe Christians. For a thorough study in the meaning of the term *disciple,* see Michael J. Wilkins, *Following the Master: A Biblical Theology of Discipleship* (Grand Rapids: Zondervan, 1992).
6. *The State of Discipleship,* 35.
7. *The State of Disciplehip,* 36.
8. David Kinnaman, *You Lost Me: Why Young Christians Are Leaving the Church . . . and Rethinking Faith* (Grand Rapids, MI: Baker, 2011), 22.
9. Thom Rainer and Sam S. Rainer III, *Essential Church? Reclaiming a Generation of Dropouts* (Nashville: B&H Publishing, 2008), 4, cited in Drew Dyck, *Generation Ex-Christian: Why Young Adults Are Leaving the Faith . . . and How to Bring them Back* (Chicago: Moody Press, 2010), 17.

10. David Kinnaman and Gabe Lyons, *UnChristian: What a New Generation Really Thinks about Christianity . . . and Why It Matters* (Grand Rapids, MI: Baker, 2007), 23

11. Rodney Stark, cited in Dyck, *Generation Ex-Christian*, 187.

12. See Peter Steinfels, "A Challenge for Churches: Adulthood Takes Its Time," *The New York Times,* December 8, 2007, www.nytimes.com/2007/12/08/us/08beliefs.html?pagewanted=print&_r=0.

13. On the current climate of Christianity and culture, see the recent and excellent book by David Kinnaman and Gabe Lyons, *Good Faith: Being a Christian When Society Thinks You're Irrelevant and Extreme* (Grand Rapids, MI: Baker, 2016).

14. Kinnaman, *You Lost Me*, 21.

15. "Faith in Flux: Changes in Religious Affiliation in the U.S." Pew Forum on Religion and Public Life, April 21, 2009, http://pewforum.org/PublicationPage.aspx?id=1154, cited in Gabe Lyons, *The Next Christians* (Colorado Springs: Multnomah, 2010), 22–23.

16. Kinnaman, *You Lost Me*, 116. Another 31 percent said that church was boring; 24 percent said their church didn't prepare them for real life.

17. Josh Packard and Ashleigh Hope, *Church Refugees: Sociologists Reveal Why People are DONE with Church but Not Their Faith* (Littleton, CO: Group Publishing, 2015).

18. Packard and Hope, *Church Refugees,* 61.

19. Packard and Hope, *Church Refugees,* 133.

20. Cited in John S. Dickerson, *The Great Evangelical Recession: Six Factors That Will Crash the American Church . . . and How to Prepare* (Grand Rapids, MI: Baker, 2013), 29.

21. American Religious Identification Survey statistics: Barry A. Kosmin and Ariela Keysar, ARIS 2008 (Hartford, CT: Trinity College, 2008), 3, cited in Lyons, *The Next Christians*, 5.

22. John Dickerson surveys four highly credible studies that all conclude that the percentage of genuine Christians—not just those who claim to be born again—is 7–9 percent; see Dickerson, *The Great Evangelical Recession*, 27–34.

23. Ed Stetzer, "The Epidemic of Biblical Illiteracy in Our Churches," *The Exchange,* July 6, 2015, http://www.christianitytoday.com/edstetzer/2015/july/epidemic-of-bible-illiteracy-in-our-churches.html.

24. A biblical worldview is defined by Barna as "believing that absolute moral truth exists; the Bible is totally accurate in all of the principles it teaches; Satan is considered to be a real being or force, not merely symbolic; a person cannot earn their way into Heaven by trying to be good or do good works; Jesus Christ lived a sinless life on earth; and God is the all-knowing, all-powerful creator of the world who still rules the universe today. In the research, anyone who held all of those beliefs was said to have a biblical

worldview." Ed Stetzer, "Barna: How Many Have a Biblical Worldview?"
The Exchange, March 9, 2009, http://www.christianitytoday.com
/edstetzer/2009/march/barna-how-many-have-biblical-worldview.html.

25. Stetzer, "Barna: How Many Have a Biblical Worldview?"
26. George Barna and Mark Hatch, *Boiling Point: How Coming Cultural Shifts Will Change Your Life* (Ventura, CA: Regal, 2001), 90.
27. "Indeed, Allah will not change the condition of a people until they change what is in themselves" (Al-Ra'd, 13:11).

CHAPTER 2—GOD'S SCANDALOUS DELIGHT: HOW GRACE MAKES US MORE LIKE JESUS

1. Eugene Peterson, *A Long Obedience in the Same Direction: Discipleship in an Instant Society* (Downers Grove, IL: InterVarsity, 2000), 133.
2. Jonathan Dodson, *Gospel-Centered Discipleship* (Wheaton, IL: Crossway, 2012), 18 (emphasis in the original).
3. I changed "you" to "me" in this rendition of Philippians 2:13.
4. George Barna and David Kinnaman, eds., *Churchless* (Carol Stream, IL: Tyndale Momentum, 2014), 80.
5. "Christians: More Like Jesus or Pharisees?" June 3, 2013, http://www .barna.org/faith-spirituality/619-are-christians-more-like-jesus-or-more-like-the-pharisees#.VpfRuTaJnww.
6. Dodson, *Gospel-Centered Discipleship,* 36.
7. Dodson, *Gospel-Centered Discipleship,* 40.
8. David Kinnaman, *You Lost Me: Why Young Christians Are Leaving the Church . . . and Rethinking Faith* (Grand Rapids, MI: Baker, 2011), 190.
9. *The State of Discipleship,* 90.
10. Dodson, *Gospel-Centered Discipleship,* 64–65.
11. Ibid.
12. Ibid., 40.

CHAPTER 3—YOU CAN'T BECOME LIKE JESUS ALONE: AUTHENTIC RELATIONSHIPS IN DISCIPLESHIP

1. David Kinnaman, *You Lost Me: Why Young Christians Are Leaving the Church . . . and Rethinking Faith* (Grand Rapids, MI: Baker, 2011), 12–13.
2. Particularly fascinating is the Reveal study done on Willow Creek Community Church, which showed that its many programs have not been producing the Christlike growth they thought. Greg L. Hawkins and Cally Parkinson, *Reveal* (South Barrington, IL: Willow Creek Association, 2007).
3. Kinnaman, *You Lost Me,* 28–29, 120.
4. *The State of Discipleship: A Barna Report Produced in Partnership with The Navigators* (2015), 87.
5. See the blog by pastor Benjamin Corey that went viral a few years ago: "10 Reasons Why People Leave the Church," August 7, 2013, http://www

.patheos.com/blogs/formerlyfundie/10-reasons-why-people-leave-church. Of the top ten reasons that pastor Corey lists, at least five (perhaps seven) have to do with relationships.

6. See Christopher Ash's fantastic and incredibly thorough book *Marriage: Sex in the Service of God* (Vancouver: Regent College Publishing, 2005).

7. See, for example, 1 Corinthians 7:1-40; Ephesians 5:21-33; and the Song of Songs.

8. The classic example, of course, is David and Jonathan. We also see examples of intimate friendships between Jesus and John, Elijah and Elisha, and Paul and several of his coworkers, including Timothy, Titus, Priscilla, Aquila, and Barnabas.

9. See Greg Ogden, *Transforming Discipleship: Making Disciples a Few at a Time* (Downers Grove, IL: InterVarsity, 2003), 59–74.

CHAPTER 4—GOD IN US (NOT JUST YOU): THE FULLNESS OF GOD IN COMMUNITY

1. Jonathan Dodson, *Gospel-Centered Discipleship* (Wheaton, IL: Crossway, 2012), 108.

2. *The State of Discipleship*, 45.

3. *The State of Discipleship*, 85

4. Dodson, *Gospel-Centered Discipleship*, 107.

5. Bill Hull, *The Complete Book of Discipleship: On Being and Making Followers of Christ* (Colorado Springs: NavPress, 2006), 67.

6. Greg Ogden, *Transforming Discipleship: Making Disciples a Few at a Time* (Downers Grove, IL: InterVarsity Press, 2003), 31.

7. *The State of Discipleship*, 87.

8. Sherry Turkle, *Alone Together: Why We Expect More from Technology and Less from Each Other* (New York: Basic Books, 2012), 1.

9. Giles Slade, *The Big Disconnect: The Story of Technology and Loneliness* (Amherst, NY: Prometheus Books, 2012).

10. *The State of Discipleship*, 87.

11. Robert Putnam, *Bowling Alone: The Collapse and Revival of American Community* (New York: Simon and Schuster, 2001).

12. Josh Packard and Ashleigh Hope, *Church Refugees: Sociologists Reveal Why People are DONE with Church but Not Their Faith* (Littleton, CO: Group Publishing, 2015), 61.

13. Packard and Hope, *Church Refugees*, 82.

14. Dodson, *Gospel-Centered Discipleship*, 108.

CHAPTER 5—ON EARTH AS IT IS IN HEAVEN

1. "Barry" is a composite figure based on several Christian business owners I've known over the years. While the specifics do not come from one particular life story, the general thrust of Barry's business does.

2. For an excellent overview of this idea, see Nancy Pearcey, *Total Truth: Liberating Christianity from Its Cultural Captivity* (Wheaton, IL: Crossway, 2004).

3. *The State of Discipleship*, 46.

4. *The State of Discipleship*, 88.

5. David Kinnaman, *You Lost Me: Why Young Christians Are Leaving the Church . . . and Rethinking Faith* (Grand Rapids, MI: Baker, 2011), 75.

6. Ibid., 140.

7. Ibid., 101.

8. Ibid., 101 (emphasis added).

9. *The State of Discipleship*, 35.

10. Ibid., 36.

11. For solid look at this theme, see Tim Keller, *Every Good Endeavor: Connecting Your Work to God's Work* (New York: Riverhead Books, 2014). For a super compelling and rather artsy treatment, see John Mark Comer's *Garden City: Work, Rest, and the Art of Being Human* (Grand Rapids, MI: Zondervan, 2015).

12. Quoted from Kuyper's inaugural address at the dedication of the Free University, which can be found in James D. Bratt, ed., *Abraham Kuyper: A Centennial Reader* (Grand Rapids, MI: Eerdmans, 1998), 488.

13. John Mark Comer, "Garden City" sermon series, accessed February 29, 2016, http://bridgetown.ajesuschurch.org/teaching/work-series/the-garden-city/.

14. Kinnaman, *You Lost Me*, 207.

15. *The State of Discipleship*, 57.

16. Ibid., 59.

17. Josh Packard and Ashleigh Hope, *Church Refugees: Sociologists Reveal Why People Are DONE with Church but Not Their Faith* (Littleton, CO: Group Publishing, 2015), 96.

18. Ibid., 122–125.

19. Ibid., 122.

20. Ibid., 123.

CHAPTER 6—LOVING GOD WITH YOUR MIND

1. *The State of Discipleship*, 91.

2. Michael J. Wilkins, *Following the Master* (Grand Rapids, MI: Zondervan, 1992), 72–73.

3. Mark Noll, *The Scandal of the Evangelical Mind* (Grand Rapids, MI: Eerdmans, 1995).

4. Mark Noll, "The Evangelical Mind Today," *First Things*, October 2004, accessed February 29, 2016, at http://www.firstthings.com/article/2004/10/the-evangelical-mind-today.

5. Walter Martin, quoted in Drew Dyck, *Generation Ex-Christian* (Chicago: Moody Press, 2010), 101.

6. Packard and Hope, *Church Refugees*, 81.

7. Dyck, *Generation Ex-Christian*, 36.

8. David Kinnaman, *You Lost Me: Why Young Christians Are Leaving the Church . . . and Rethinking Faith* (Grand Rapids, MI: Baker, 2011), 127.

9. See Matthew 16:5-28; Luke 18:1-43; John 21:15-19.

10. Greg Ogden, *Transforming Discipleship: Making Disciples a Few at a Time* (Downers Grove, IL: InterVarsity Press, 2003), 89.

11. Ogden, *Transforming Discipleship*, 89.

12. See Clinton Arnold, "Early Church Catechesis and New Christians' Classes in Contemporary Evangelicalism," Journal of the Evangelical Theological Society 47 (2004): 39–54, accessed February 29, 2016, at http://www.etsjets.org/files/JETS-PDFs/47/47-1/47-1-pp039-054_JETS.pdf.

13. The first of several posts was called "Intersex and Christian Theology," October 13, 2015, http://www.patheos.com/blogs/theologyintheraw/2015/10/intersex-and-christian-theology/.

14. Dan Kimball, *They Like Jesus but Not the Church: Insights from Emerging Generations* (Grand Rapids, MI: Zondervan, 2007), 218.

CHAPTER 7—MISSION: NOT JUST MORALITY

1. Brandon Hatmaker, *Barefoot Church: Serving the Least in a Consumer Culture* (Grand Rapids, MI: Zondervan, 2011), 78.

2. See Hatmaker, *Barefoot Church*, 74–78.

3. Josh Packard and Ashleigh Hope, *Church Refugees: Sociologists Reveal Why People Are DONE with Church but Not Their Faith* (Littleton, CO: Group Publishing, 2015), 21.

4. Packard and Hope, *Church Refugees*, 104.

5. George Barna and David Kinnaman, eds., *Churchless* (Carol Stream, IL: Tyndale Mometum, 2014), 42.

6. David Kinnaman, *You Lost Me: Why Young Christians Are Leaving the Church . . . and Rethinking Faith* (Grand Rapids, MI: Baker, 2011), 114.

7. Ibid., 119.

8. Austin New Church (ANC) started doing this several years ago. See Hatmaker, *Barefoot Church*, 119–121.

9. This phrase is from Packard and Hope, *Church Refugees*.

10. Joshua Ryan Butler told me this in an e-mail on January 14, 2016.

11. Check it out. It's an awesome ministry: http://projectbayview.com.

12. Kimball, *They Like Jesus but Not the Church*, 20.

CHAPTER 8—THE MOST SEGREGATED HOUR OF THE WEEK

1. Cited in Mark DeYmaz, *HUP: Should Pastors Accept or Reject the Homogeneous Unit Principle?* (Dallas: Leadership Network, 2012), 14.

2. Martin Luther King said this in a speech at Western Michigan University on December 18, 1963: "We must face the fact that in America, the church is still the most segregated major institution in America. At eleven o'clock on Sunday morning when we stand and sing and Christ has no east or west, we stand at the most segregated hour in this nation. This is tragic. Nobody of honesty can overlook this."

3. Bob Smietana, "Sunday Morning Segregation," *Christianity Today*, January 15, 2015, http://www.christianitytoday.com/gleanings/2015/january /sunday-morning-segregation-most-worshipers-church-diversity.html.

4. See Jarvis Williams, "Racial Reconciliation, the Gospel, and the Church," September 25, 2015, http://9marks.org/article/racial-reconciliation-the -gospel-and-the-church/.

5. See Ken L. Davis, "Designing Worship for Multiethnic Churches (Part One)," *Journal of Ministry and Theology* (Spring 2004), accessed March 4, 2016, http://www.summitu.edu/Assets/uploads/Summit/import /www.bbc.edu/journal/volume8_1/designing_multicultural_worship.pdf.

6. For an excellent defense of what I argue in this chapter, see Rodney Woo, *The Color of Church: A Biblical and Practical Paradigm for Multiracial Churches* (Nashville: B&H Academic, 2009); J. Daniel Hays, *From Every People and Nation: A Biblical Theology of Race* (Downers Grove, IL: IVP Academic, 2003); Jarvis Williams, *One New Man: The Cross and Racial Reconciliation in Pauline Theology* (Nashville: B&H Academic, 2010); Derwin Gray, *The High-Definition Leader: Building Multiethnic Churches in a Multiethnic World* (Nashville: Thomas Nelson, 2015). Or a great place to start is the series of articles put out by 9 Marks in summer/fall 2015: http://9marks.org/journal/multi-ethnic-churches/.

7. While racism is the belief that one's race is superior to others, ethnocentrism is the tendency to look at the world through one's own cultural perspective. The subtlety of ethnocentrism comes when you believe, like the racist, that your ethnicity is superior.

8. See Dan Kimball's eye-opening chapter titled "The Church Is Dominated by Males and Oppresses Females," in *They Like Jesus but Not the Church* (Grand Rapids, MI: Zondervan, 2007), 115–135.

9. See for instance Deuteronomy 32:11-12; Isaiah 42:14; Hosea 11:3-4; 49:15; 66:13; Matthew 23:37.

10. See the incisive book by Derwin Gray, *The High-Definition Leader: Building Multiethnic Churches in a Multiethnic World* (Nashville: Thomas Nelson, 2015).

11. Adam Dachis, "Fish Don't Know They're in Water," July 14, 2011, http:// lifehacker.com/5821126/fish-dont-know-theyre-in-water.

12. My friend Derwin Gray, a pastor at one of America's largest multiethnic churches, confirmed this point I'm making. Which is reassuring, since he's been doing multiethnic ministry for a couple decades.

13. Paul talks about justification by faith in Romans 3:21-26; 4:1-6; 5:8-11; Galatians 2:16-21; 3:6-12, 22-26; and Philippians 3:6-9 (implicitly). He mentions justification by faith in three of his thirteen letters. Paul talks about the Jerusalem collection in Romans 15:25-33; 1 Corinthians 16:1-4; 2 Corinthians 8:1-9:15; and Galatians 2:10. This doesn't include the various places where he talks about churches supporting his missionary endeavors (Romans 16:2; Philippians 4:14-20) and a passage in Acts that talks about the financial need in Jerusalem (Acts 11:27-30).

CHAPTER 9—A MORE SIMPLE WAY

1. Five million children die every year because of hunger and malnutrition. There are 8,765 hours in a year, which means 570 children die every hour. Assuming it'll take you about twenty to thirty minutes to read this chapter . . .

2. See George Barna and Frank Viola, *Pagan Christianity? Exploring the Roots of Our Church Practices,* 3rd ed. (Carol Stream, IL: Tyndale, 2012), 41. Since I cite this highly controversial book, I should add that while I resonate with many things that Barna and Viola talk about and find their overall analysis of the church to be thought-provoking, if not on the mark, there are several things I disagree with and find to be overstated, inaccurate, and worded in a somewhat condescending tone. I'll spare you the details, but if you're familiar with the book, I just want you to know that I haven't uncritically drunk the punch.

3. Rich Stearns, *The Hole in Our Gospel* (Nashville: Thomas Nelson, 2009), 216.

4. Josh Packard and Ashleigh Hope, *Church Refugees: Sociologists Reveal Why People Are Done with Church but Not Their Faith* (Loveland, CO: Group Publishing, 2015), 71. See also p. 96.

5. Along with the statistics in *The State of Discipleship*, see Brandon Hatmaker, *Barefoot Church* (Grand Rapids, MI: Zondervan, 2011), 99–117.

6. I don't love the word *tithe,* since it literally means giving one tenth of your income, which is nowhere mandated in the New Testament. But since the word *tithe* is the common term used for "giving money toward ministry," I'll keep using it in this chapter, despite its literal meaning.

7. This is the whole point of 2 Corinthians 8–9, where Paul praises the churches in Greece and Asia Minor for helping the poor believers in Jerusalem.

8. One of my favorite stripped-down churches is Austin New Church in Texas (the church Brandon Hatmaker helped start). Or the Church under the Bridge that meets—you guessed it—under a bridge in Waco.

AFTERWORD

1. Doug Nuenke, ed., *Five Traits of a Christ-Follower* (Colorado Springs: NavPress, 2015), xii–xiii.

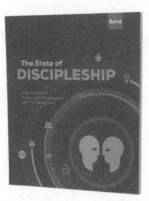

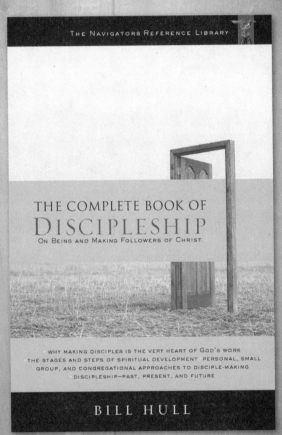